Also by Brad Kessler

Birds in Fall

Lick Creek

The Woodcutter's Christmas

GOAT SONG

A Seasonal Life,
A Short History of Herding, and
the Art of Making Cheese

BRAD KESSLER

Scribner
New York London Toronto Sydney

SCRIBNER
A Division of Simon & Schuster, Inc.
1230 Avenue of the Americas
New York, NY 10020

First Scribner hardcover edition June 2009

Designed by Kyoko Watanabe

Photographs by Dona Ann McAdams

Manufactured in the United States of America

10 9 8 7 6 5 4

Library of Congress Cataloging-in-Publication Data

Kessler, Brad.
Goat song : a seasonal life, a short history of herding, and the art of making cheese / Brad Kessler.
p. cm.
1. Goats—Vermont. 2. Goatherds—Vermont. 3. Goat cheese—Vermont.
I. Title.
SF383.K47 2009
636.3'9009743—dc22
2009001651

ISBN 978-1-4165-6099-9
ISBN 978-1-4165-6115-6 (ebook)

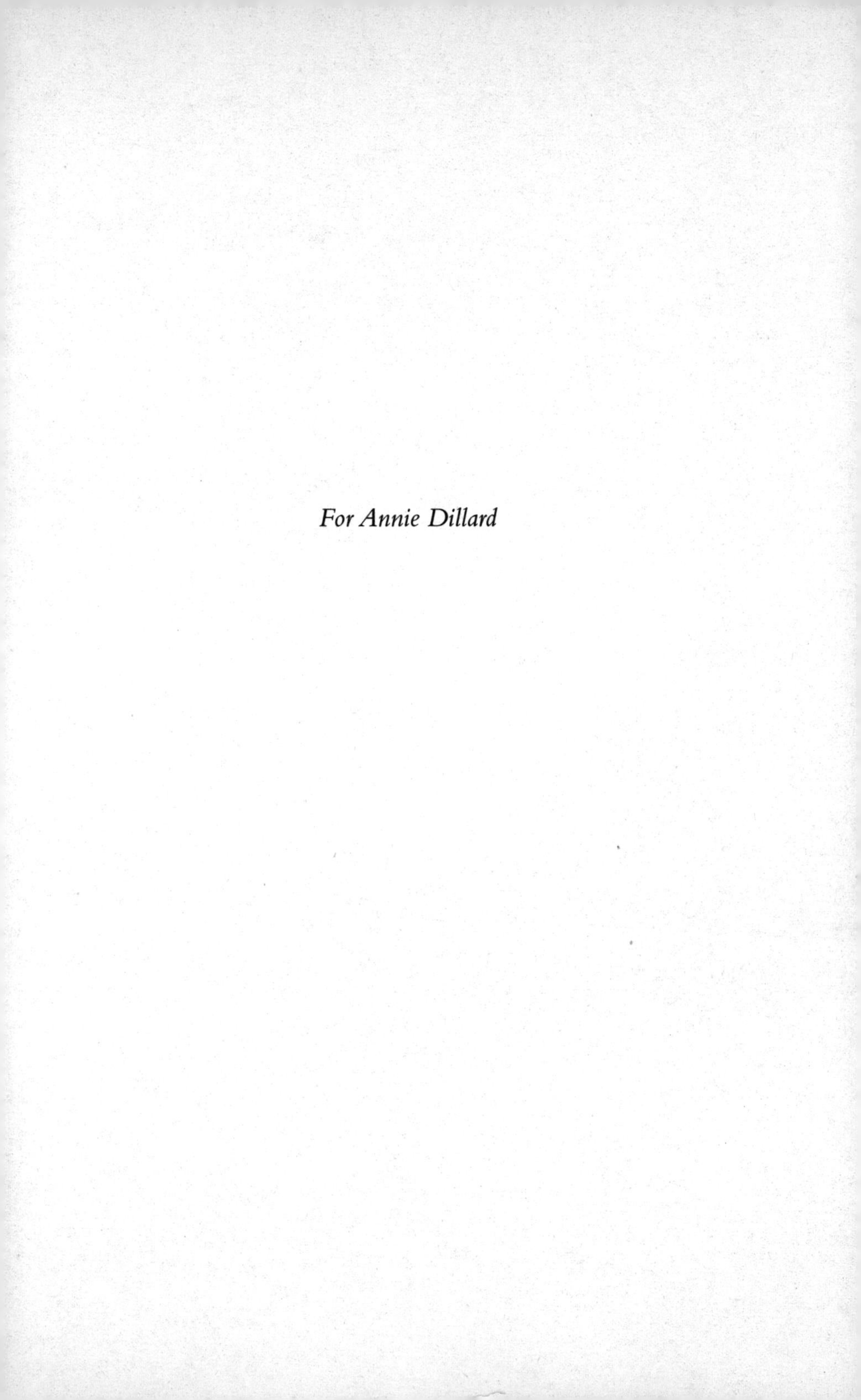

For Annie Dillard

GOAT SONG

Shepherd. *They say that on your barren mountain ridge*
You have measured out the road that the soul treads
When it has vanished from our natural eyes;
That you have talked with apparitions.

Goatherd. *Indeed*
My daily thoughts since the first stupor of youth
Have found the path my goats' feet cannot find.

Shepherd. *Sing, for it may be that your thoughts have plucked*
Some medicable herb to make our grief
Less bitter.

—W. B. YEATS

PART I

Birth

Prologue

Early June. The mountains turn tender green this time of year, the skies become enamel blue. The goats wear bells around their necks while we hike up Mason's Hill. There's eight of us here today—seven goats, one human. We step through salad greens and the goats taste everything in sight: steeplebush, wild strawberries, buttercups, blackberry vines. We're heading to the mountains soon.

Each day we wander the Vermont woods for an hour or two. I love the leave-taking, the sound of the goats' bells, the brief nomadism. Herding is a way of doing something while doing nothing; it asks only for one's presence, awake, watching animals and earth.

Wind rakes the trees. Clouds float shadows through the grass. We enter the woods and the goats eat ash, birch, and maple. This evening I'll milk the does back in the barn and when the sun goes down I'll make an aged cheese from their milk called a *tomme*. Months from now when snow covers the mountains, I'll open that *tomme* and find this day again inside its rind: the aromatic grass, the leaves, this wind.

I call the goats on. They moan back from their branches.

Hannah and Lizzie, Pie and Nisa, Penny, Eustace, and Alice—I know each voice as well as any human's. We're heading up the slope now. They nod through cinnamon ferns.

A goat path in the wild leads to mountaintops where other animals can't go. Some afternoons I follow my goats and others they follow me. The Igbo of Nigeria tell their children, if lost in the wilderness follow a goat, she always knows the way back home. I've been following these goats back home each day, but where they lead surprises me still.

I want to take you there.

Beginnings

YEARS AGO I FELL IN LOVE WITH A FARMHOUSE IN West Virginia. The house sat at the head of a hollow—wide-board floors, a rusted tin roof—the last outpost before impassable mountains. You drove up a dirt road beside a murmuring creek and came to a cattle gate. When you hooked the gate again it felt like you were leaving the world behind.

I lived in Manhattan back then but never felt right in the city. I longed for fewer people and more trees. The rented farmhouse was an anodyne. Between semesters and on long weekends my wife, Dona, and I escaped to West Virginia. I adored the long drives, the eight-hour commute, the layers of Manhattan peeling away with each Mid-Atlantic state—New Jersey, Pennsylvania, Maryland, Virginia. It felt like stripping out of formal attire; by the Alleghenies we were down to underwear.

We were about to shake hands on the West Virginia farmhouse when a phone call came one night. The seller had burned down the house. Turned out he never really owned the homeplace—his sister did. He burned the house for spite. A family feud. An Appalachian story. The night the call came

I mourned, convinced we'd never find such a perfect place again.

My whole life it seemed I'd been searching for a retreat in the mountains, a patch of land where I could grow my own food. I was a writer, Dona a photographer. We made our living—our art—with paper but we longed to make it with earth as well. Ever since reading *Walden* as a teen I'd nursed Thoreau's old dream of self-reliance, his cabin along the lake, his meticulous lists of peas and beans. I admired how he wove literary culture and agriculture into one fabric—pen in one hand, hoe in the other—and how he understood that alongside civil disobedience, the most active thing one could do on earth was produce one's own food.

For five years we searched for a home. We scoured the whole Northeast, looked at a hundred plots of land. One week a realtor called from Vermont. He'd found an eighteenth-century farmhouse on a dead-end road in the western part of the state. The asking price was absurdly low; the farmhouse had sat empty for years and nothing inside was expected to work. We might have to tear the place down, he confessed, and start anew. Yet the land was apparently stunning, worth the asking price alone. There was an orchard, a pond, outbuildings, a brook. Seventy-five acres of sheepland grown back to forest.

We drove there late one October afternoon when the trees had shed their leaves. The valley looked promising; narrow and forested with folded hills. An opalescent river tumbled aside the road. The pavement turned to gravel, then we jostled up a rocky drive and the house swung into view: bone white clapboards, mountains all around. We both knew right away.

•

This was over a decade ago. Back then neither of us knew much about animal husbandry (we'd both grown up in the suburbs). But soon Dona began photographing neighboring dairy farms and helping with chores; and that led to a familiarity—a friendship—with animals, particularly with goats.

This is the story of our first years with dairy goats. A story about what it's like to live with animals who directly feed you. I tell of cheese and culture and agriculture, but also of the rediscovery of a pastoral life. *Rediscovery* because the longer I lived with goats the more connections I saw to a collective human past we've since forgotten, here in North America at least. I saw how so many aspects of our everyday culture—from our alphabet to our diet to elements of our economy and poetry—arose from a lifestyle of herding hoofed animals, and how unbeknownst to most of us, pastoralism still informs so much of the way we live today.

Goats had intrigued me for years—their intelligence, their seeming disdain of human dominion. I once trailed a herd of goats in India through the Thar Desert back to their homes at night. A herder led them into the walled city of Jaisalmer. The goats marched single file, hoofs clicking cobbles, while scooters and trucks squeezed past. At each narrow curve another doe broke from the parade and turned in to a home where a member of the household—a child or a woman—held open a wooden door and greeted the returning goat with a palmful of salt. The does had returned from the desert to be milked and bedded with their family at night. In the morning they'd gather again with the herder. I'd never seen such a wonderful arrangement before—goats and humans living side by side—but it was one of the most ancient continuous relationships between mammals.

In Vermont, Dona milked a neighbor's goats when the neighbor went away. She brought home the raw milk still warm in a glass bottle. I made a *queso blanco,* the simplest cheese in the world. (You heat the milk, add a spoonful of vinegar, and the curds separate from the whey like magic; drain the curds in a cheesecloth, let them drip for a few minutes and—*voilà*—you've made a cheese.) The *queso blanco* was tasty but a bit rubbery. When the neighbor went away again I tried my hand at making chèvre. I had a small bottle of rennet and the right starter culture. The curds set up overnight and the next day I drained them in a cheesecloth. When we tried the fresh chèvre the following afternoon, it tasted like nothing we'd ever eaten before—a custard, a creamy pudding, the cheese so young and floral it held within its curd the taste of grass and herbs the goat had eaten the day before. It seemed we were eating not a cheese, but a meadow.

The French used to call cheese "the drunkard's biscuit." That afternoon we were intoxicated without drinking a thing. We devoured the creamy chèvre smeared on slices of bread, ran fingers across the plate. We couldn't understand why it tasted so good. Was it the raw unpasteurized milk, or that we knew the goats—their labor and ours? "Who has not sometimes derived an inexpressible satisfaction from his food, in which appetite had no share?" wrote Thoreau. "I have been inspired through the palate."

That afternoon we decided: it was time to get our goats.

Yearlings

Begin, my muses, begin
the herdsman's song

—THEOCRITUS, *IDYLLS*

MARY BETH BOLDUC LOOKED EVERY BIT THE MILKMAID: rust-colored curls, porcelain arms, eggshell blue eyes. We'd met her in the driveway to her farm. She was a chemist and cheesemaker who lived across the border in New York State. We'd come to her farm to choose four goats from her herd. It was May and the lilacs were in bloom. Mary Beth swung open the metal gate to her paddock. She was wearing green Wellington boots.

Mary Beth raised American Nubian goats. She bred them not only for the butterfat in their milk—good for cheese—but for their size. Hers were large goats, tall, long-legged—*ladylike* was her term. They stood on a hill in her field, twelve does and one enormous buck, each copper or ecru with black spots or stripes or airbrushed belts of caramel and white. Long white ears framed their faces like large parentheses. They all had white topknots, as if someone had squirted Reddi-wip on each one's head. They were not like the goats I learned about as a child, the ragged white and bearded nanny and billy who licked tin cans. These were all coffee and cream and mocha. Elegant creatures. Enchanting. They'd all been disbudded—dehorned—which was safer but sad. How magnificent they'd have looked with crowns of horns.

The sun dipped from a cloud and bathed them in amber. A watercolor of goats. We could hear newborn kids calling from the barn.

We wanted to start our herd slowly, with two kids and two yearlings, and gradually build our numbers. The thirteen-month-old yearlings would be ready to breed that fall; which meant, with any luck, by next spring they'd birth their own kids—and we'd then have milk.

Mary Beth ushered us into her barn. A swarm of kids rushed the gate. They bleated and nickered and pooled around our legs, lifted tiny hoofs to our knees. Mary Beth bottle-raised them all, which explained their excitement over us. They followed us around like puppies—a tide of wagging tails.

Dona squatted and a kid leaped into her lap. A small one sucked my finger. Most were brown but one sported white polka dots and another was eggplant black with a buttery undercarriage—she looked like an Italian loafer. Mary Beth had saved these two for us; she knew Dona worked in black and white.

I went outside to look at the yearlings. The does were grazing down the hill. They raised heads and watched as I approached. The yearlings were easy to tell from the adults: smaller, with twiggy legs, a teenage awkwardness. A pair broke from the pack and loped toward me. One was golden with a satin coat; the other mahogany with orange and black face stripes. Their long white ears flapped when they trotted. They ran across the meadow like flying nuns.

The golden doe shoved her head into my palm and demanded a scratch. The mahogany turned her face toward mine. The golden doe closed her eyes and made an odd purring sound. The mahogany one studied me, unconvinced.

I walked. They followed. The golden doe rubbed her head against the mahogany's neck; the mahogany reared on hind legs and crashed down toward the other's head: an invitation to play. Then they both reared in perfect choreography and balanced on back legs and twisted heads to the right. For a second their forelegs hung suspended in the air, then they crashed down skull to skull. You could hear the knock of bones, like billiard balls.

When they had enough play the golden doe came over for another scratch, then they browsed again. Halfway back to the barn they exploded into an epileptic run. They kicked legs out to the sides, flung heads, spun bodies. A caper. A capriole. I never really saw where the words came from but now their origin was clear: *capra,* the goat.

In the dark of the barn Dona and Mary Beth were bottle-feeding kids.

"So," Mary Beth asked with a grin. "Did you choose any goats?"

No, I said, I hadn't; but two of them had chosen me.

The golden doe was registered with the American Dairy Goat Association as "Tuffins'—Meadow Hannah," the mahogany with the face stripes as "Tuffins'—Meadow Lizzie." Tattoo numbers AN1352274 and AN1352276 respectively. They were half sisters, sired by the same father (Galloup-n-Bootleg Speakeasy) and out of different mothers (Alice-of-Jewel and

Zoey). The two newborn kids hadn't yet been registered or named.

We handed Mary Beth seven hundred dollars that afternoon. She'd keep the four goats until we were ready. First we needed to build a fence and barn. The difficult part was about to begin.

Pasture

An apple orchard lay to the side of our house. Twelve Northern Spys with mossed bark and sapsucker holes. The trees hadn't been pruned in decades and the apples they bore came wrinkled and deformed, the size of infants' fists.

The orchard was the best place for a pasture: three acres of untamed fescue, clover, and goldenrod. Norway spruces encircled the spot. Given enough winters the goats would likely rim the apple trees, but that was the sacrifice we made: milk instead of Northern Spys.

All summer we ran fencing. I split locust posts, cleared brush, dug holes with a posthole digger. Every spare moment I spent in the orchard closing in the acreage with welded wire fence. Goats are notorious escape artists and everyone in the valley had a story (most of them untrue) about how goats could unlatch gates, leap six-foot fences, eat tires off of cars. The fence was less about keeping goats in than keeping other animals out: dogs, bobcats, bears. Especially coyotes. The valley echoed on summer nights with their howls.

The welded wire came in one-hundred-foot lengths. I

humped the four-foot scrolls up hills and rolled them out like carpets in the grass. Dona held the running fence against trees while I pulled the wire with a come-along, then hammered it in place with two-inch fence staples. Spruce sap tarred our hands; sweat stung our eyes. Some evenings we worked long into dusk, when the hermit thrush sang in the woods, and the late sun reddened the fencing and gave the orchard an unexpectedly ordered look. A fence changes everything, makes an inside and an out, and suddenly a paddock appeared before us, a three-acre room where none had been before. It gave me pleasure to see, as if we'd made a tiny world anew.

An old chicken coop served as our barn. We cleared out rusted paint cans, guano, fishing rods. An ancient scythe, the delicate bleached bones of mice. I built a gate and sectioned off a part for milking and cut a door in the back leading to the paddock. We capped the crumbling roof with tin. *All this,* I thought, *for cheese?*

By first frost we still hadn't finished the fencing and the gates had yet to be hung. It was already mid-October by the time we finally headed back to Mary Beth's farm. We laid the backseat of the old Saab down and lined it with a tarp and a broken bale of hay. At Mary Beth's place, Dona buckled collars around the yearlings' necks—Hannah the golden doe, Lizzie the mahogany. Leaves hurled across the grass. Mary Beth lured the goats toward the car with apples. I helped her haul one doe and then the other into the hatch—each weighed about 130 pounds. Dona bundled the two small kids inside a dog crate and closed the wire door. They were the size of miniature greyhounds, and fit inside the crate with extra room.

The rest of the herd had come down to watch. They maundered softly across the fence. Hannah and Lizzie pressed faces against the car window and bleated. Somewhere in that crowd were their mothers, sisters, brothers, aunts, grandmothers. Would they miss them? Mary Beth stood by the gate and waved goodbye.

Out on the paved road, the yearlings settled. Hannah folded her front legs like a camel and sat. Lizzie did the same. Hannah laid her chin over the armrest and watched the landscape. Lizzie put her head on her sister's back. The two kids slept inside their crate. Rain came in spurts. We couldn't believe their calm; it seemed the does had been chauffeured around their entire lives. Hannah soon stretched her neck and began to chew her cud. Lizzie did too. The wipers slapped and the road turned black with rain.

Herd

THEY WERE A NEW HERD IN A NEW PASTURE AND WE were new herders—we all had so much to learn. That first afternoon we walked the four goats around the orchard. Lizzie stared across the lawn. Hannah moaned. The kids looked left to right. The grass was wet but the sky had cleared, and the does searched everywhere for the herd they'd left behind.

We brought them into the barn. Each investigated the iron manger, the newly painted walls. They raised and lowered heads, sniffed at everything. Their hackles rose when they saw the big black poodle. Lola was as astonished as they. Lizzie with the face stripes tried to butt the dog through the fence.

In the wild, when frightened, goats climb to the highest peak for safety. After dark that first night the does climbed the tallest hill in the paddock. Three times I found them with the flashlight in the dark, silent and bunched together in the woods. They followed me back to the barn, but a few minutes later, they ran back up the hill in fear. Finally I locked them inside; they'd have to get used to their new home sooner or later.

The next few days whenever we emerged from the house—to let the dog out or hang laundry or walk to the garden or garage—the goats screamed. We'd been warned: Nubians are the loudest of the domestic goat breeds and the cry of a goat is so haunting and dramatic our word *tragedy* comes from it: *tragōidia* in Greek—the cry of the goat. The goat song. It sounded as if the new goats were being skinned alive.

I fell for their histrionics at first; their faces and dangling ears pressed against the fence were hard to resist. The moment I entered the paddock they settled down. They circled around, a ring of goats, nudged and jostled and burrowed heads into my palm. I gave them a scratch, a rub, eight amber eyes turned up at me. If they couldn't have their larger herd, they at least wanted us.

The days were lovely then, cool and sere. The mountains hung with red and golden leaves. At first light I lugged a bale of hay up to the barn, broke flakes into the mangers, filled water buckets. The does would already be at pasture. I'd tell Lola, "Go get the goats," and the black poodle would race up the hill and find them, and soon they'd all spill down the hill, leaping and twirling, hooting, flying up and banking off a picnic table we'd placed in their paddock. Then we all climbed back up the hill together and the does ran beneath the Northern Spys. They balanced on back legs to reach hanging boughs, or used my chest for a leg-up. I knocked apples off limbs with a long stick, and the does chased them down and fought one another for the fruit. Lola watched for another prize. A goat's anus would open like the aperture of a camera and produce perfectly round pellets, one by one. The dog ate them; we couldn't convince her their feces were not a treat.

"Anyone who has the care of goats," David Mackenzie

wrote in his 1957 classic, *Goat Husbandry,* "soon grows to realize that the relationship between the goatherd and his flock is a great deal more personal, more intimate and more delicate than is usual in the farmyard."

Personal, intimate, delicate. Those autumn afternoons I sat with the goats for hours on the hill. They gazed Talmudically across the mountains while they chewed their cud. Their breath smelled of spruce and rumen. Pie, the spotted kid, brought up a ball of cud and stood chewing like an outfielder with a pouch in her left cheek. We named her after the Gerard Manley Hopkins poem "Pied Beauty" because of her polka dots. The eggplant-black kid we named Nisa. She'd lay a small hoof on my arm until I scratched her brisket; and if I stopped she'd tap once again until I resumed. Hannah, the golden doe, came over and sniffed my ear or licked my chin. Lizzie watched the dog.

Every herd develops a hierarchy of its own, an acceptance of its members, even those at the bottom of the order. Goats establish rank by jousting, by rearing up on hind legs and crashing down horn-to-horn—or head-to-head. Usually the contests are playful, but sometimes a doe will bite or use her horns to slash or ram an inferior with bruising force. Outsiders to the herd are often picked on ruthlessly.

Hannah dominated from the start. Lizzie, her half sister, offered a little competition, but head-to-head Hannah had the weight and could sumo Lizzie aside with a thrust of her neck. Each evening the does played king of the hill on the picnic table. One would leap up on the tabletop and challenge the others. Hannah always won; no one could unseat her. She commanded the best place in the barn, right beneath the manger, a spot cushioned heavily with hay. From her throne she kept one eye on the door, the other on everyone else; and if she grew peckish she simply stretched her neck up and grabbed a mouthful of hay. In the mornings, Hannah led the herd out to pasture, and she brought them back to the barn at regular intervals during the day. Out browsing, she decided where and when the herd would stop. She'd stand on back legs and bend a sapling down with her forelegs and let the kids eat as well. She always gobbled the most apples, the most grain, the most amount of leaves.

A feral herd of goats consists of up to forty members. When the herd goes out to browse the herd queen leads and determines the course while the herd king—what David Mackenzie calls "King Billy"—takes up the rear. If Hannah was our apparent herd queen, in the absence of a resident buck, Lizzie, the mahogany doe, took the role of herd king. When we walked together in the woods, Lizzie always took the rear. While Hannah and Nisa and Pie grazed, the mahogany doe scanned the horizon. If the dog came too close, she'd step toward Lola with hackles raised and head lowered; and if Lola didn't get the message Lizzie would rear and strike. Sometimes she rammed the dog just for good measure. At twilight she patrolled outside the barn. Only when everyone else had gone in for the night did she take her position by the door. Given her constant policing, Lizzie ate the least. She was all muscle and bone.

Those October days I took the goats up Mason's Hill and walked them in the woods. Yellow leaves the size of serviettes still clung to the moosewood limbs. The goats devoured them with relish and picked still-green leaves off the honeysuckle bushes and searched for acorns. I didn't drive the goats those afternoons the way one drives sheep or cattle. I walked alongside them. The relationship between the goatherder and his goats is one of trust, not threat; when we were out together the does followed wherever I went. Even if they'd found a cache of tasty acorns I could call them off and eventually they'd come away, complaining the whole time.

Unlike cows and sheep, goats are browsers; they eat plants with woody stems and leaves. Goats will graze grass, but given the choice, they prefer to eat up high (not only for the nutritional value of leaves and bark, but also because plants off the ground harbor fewer parasites). A goat will always reach for the highest twig or leaf. They'll balance on back legs like circus dogs, or even climb the tree. On pasture sheep graze shoulder-to-shoulder, a straight line across a meadow; but goats go their own way, a loose confederation, with one eye always on the herd. If one gets separated from the others, she'll momentarily panic before she finds them again.

"The goat is much more hardy than the sheep, and in every respect more fitted to a life of liberty," wrote Thomas Bewick in his 1792 *History of the Quadrupeds*. "It chooses it own pasture, straying wherever its appetite or inclination leads. It chiefly delights in wild and mountainous regions, climbing the loftiest rocks and standing secure on the verge of inaccessible and dangerous precipices."

We lived in the mountains, but ours were gentle and green, with no dangerous precipices in sight. Yet on our walks when we came upon outcrops, the goats delighted in clambering upon them—as if they'd discovered land after years at sea. I tried to find them rocks wherever we roamed.

Like all ruminants, goats have four stomachs, the largest of which, the rumen, is a kind of fermentation vat containing thousands of microbes (bacteria and protozoa) that turn otherwise indigestible cellulose into food. When a goat goes off to browse, she fills her rumen to capacity with leaves and grass. Once sated, she retreats to a safe place—a barn or cliff or a place with a view—and in a quiet moment, usually in the company of others, she ruminates. She stretches her neck and regurgitates from her rumen a ball of partly digested cud. She chews this over and over, and the roughage further breaks down as it passes back and forth from the rumen to the reticulum. When she's thoroughly masticated the material, she'll extend her neck again—this closes a slit in the esophagus and prevents food from directly entering the rumen—and the cud drops into the third stomach, the omasum. Final digestion occurs in the abomasum, the "true" stomach, which corresponds to the single stomach of other mammals—a stomach like our own.

The arrangement of going out to browse and stuffing one's stomach and digesting later works well for ruminants who are prey animals, in constant danger from predators. It allows them to gather a lot of material out in the open and return to the safety of their citadel to digest. Since leaves and grass are 80 percent water, it means a goat must go out several times a day to gather enough raw material and nutrients to keep her healthy. A goat's day is spent ruminating, foraging, sleeping, and playing—roughly in that order.

Those mid-October days our does spent most of their mornings cudding near the barn. They lounged in the sun beside the picnic table, one leg splayed in front, the others tucked beneath. When the dew burned off the grass around eleven, they marched up the hill single file and grazed for a few hours, then returned at midday for a siesta inside the barn. Around three they foraged again for an hour; and at sundown filed out again for a long crepuscular feed. Twilight, they jousted on the picnic table or ran circles around one another and butted heads. Often we joined them in the paddock; the vesper bells from the monastery over the mountain would echo across the hills at that hour, and the wind stirred from the south. Dona brought out a currycomb and brush; and the does gathered around us in the umber dusk and pressed their heads close to receive our ministrations. "A poem should begin in delight and end in wisdom," Robert Frost said. The goats were delightful those first weeks. The wisdom—and the work—came later.

Estrus

A STARTLING NUMBER OF PEOPLE ASKED US THAT FIRST year: *When will you milk your goats?* I had to remind them of what they already knew: that a female mammal needs to have a baby *first* to lactate, that cows and goats, like humans, don't just spontaneously secrete milk. We had to breed our goats to get them pregnant to get the milk. The animal husbandry was a bit like the old Passover tune "Chad Gadya," "One Kid Goat." "Chad Gadya" is a cumulative chain song sung at the end of each Passover Seder, and every verse ends with a rousing "One kid goat!" And that's what we needed to get milk from our does: *chad gadya.*

Goats in the northern hemisphere breed in autumn. Their kids gestate for five months and are born in spring when the grass begins to grow. Shortening daylight triggers sexual rut in male goats and estrus, or heat, in females. Throughout autumn a doe goes into estrus usually once every three weeks. Her heat lasts for as little as twelve and as long as forty-eight hours. The window of estrus each time is fairly small, and only during that period will a female "stand" for a sexually active buck and allow herself to be bred. A few hours off one way or the other, the doe will take a look at an aroused buck and run (she won't "stand" for him). Bucks remain in rut throughout the fall, which means that season they're *always* willing and always—horns or not—horny.

Had we kept a resident male in our herd we could have simply turned him out with the females at that time of year and they'd all have had their way au naturel when everyone was ready. But we kept no buck because—bucks stink.

During breeding season male goats secrete a pungent pheromone from scent glands on the head and under the tail. The hot, tangy odor comes from the chemical compound 6-trans nonenal, a smell one usually associates with particularly funky (or rancid) goat cheese. Nineteenth-century European farmers kept bucks in their barns under the false belief that their odor kept illness away from other animals. Their musk has hints of burnt steel, cat piss, and teenage sneakers. Since we didn't want that fragrance around the house, we arranged to take our does to a buck instead. And if we had to chauffeur each doe to a date with a buck, we needed to know exactly when she was in heat. The window had to be, as it were, open.

I had no idea what a doe in "standing heat" looked like that first year. Each October morning I checked Hannah and Lizzie (Pie and Nisa were too young to breed that fall). Were their tails flicking? Were their vulvas engorged or oozing fluid? Were they acting odd or restless, more vocal than usual, or trying to hump each other?

I had to lift their tails to see. They didn't like my sneaking around their rears, and soon grew wary of my advances. Hannah, who'd normally come right up for a scratch, now avoided me. The moment I tried to get back there she'd flee or spin around and face me, ears back, ready to strike. Heat in virgin does is not always easy to detect, and all our does were virgins. To goat sex, so were we.

The nights soon dropped into the twenties, and the days turned bitter and gray. By mid-November the does grew winter coats. Hannah put on a luxurious golden mink, Lizzie a mahogany fur. Nisa's coat was lustrous black, and Pie's a map of the night sky: Cassiopeia. In their new furs, they looked ready for a date with the buck. Dona phoned Mary Beth Bolduc and asked how we would know precisely when the does were ready. Mary Beth told us to come next Sunday and she'd give us a "buck cloth." What was a buck cloth? Bring an empty jar and a rag, she said, and we'd see.

Pan

The wise people who created for us the idea of Pan thought that of all fears, the fear of him was the most terrible, since it embraces all.

—ROBERT LOUIS STEVENSON

SUNDAY WAS WARM FOR NOVEMBER, THE SKY THE COLOR of bleach. In Mary Beth's driveway we caught the feral scent of buck. I carried a blue washcloth for the occasion. Dona brought an empty coffee can—Chock Full o' Nuts.

Earlier that fall when Mary Beth's buck started showing signs of rut, she'd separated him from the female herd. She wanted to time the breeding of her does so they'd all deliver around the same time in early May. She'd wait for Thanksgiving morning to let her buck out; this way her does would start to kid five months later and not before.

That morning Goliath paced his wire pen. The buck was jet black and hairy with a pink tongue and long black beard—he was the sire of our kids, Nisa and Pie. At this time of year, pumped on testosterone, he could be aggressive, but in his pen he looked magnificent—and magnificently filthy. His massive neck and head bristled with oil and musk. He looked as if he'd been hanging out at Jiffy Lube.

We followed Mary Beth to his small pen. The does tagged along behind. Goliath put his front hoofs on his fence and leaned as far across the wire as he could. His eyes widened; his tongue flicked. His penis lifted, a red divining rod, pencil thin. His testicles looked like two tennis balls sewn in a velvet sack. Few mammals' gonads rival the relative size of a male goat's testes.

Mary Beth ushered us into his paddock. Goliath stepped off the fence and considered us. His musk was intense; I felt it in my lungs. Eight months of the year he didn't smell at all and he was friendly and docile, but once in rut his hormones turned him into a sex addict and a bully. He didn't particularly cozy to humans during rut, unless you were a menstruating female (in which case he'd be *very* interested). "Owners should exercise caution working around sexually active bucks," Mary Smith and David Sherman warn in their veterinary manual *Goat Medicine*. "A full-grown buck striking from the standing position can produce serious or fatal injury."

Mary Beth approached Goliath. He eyed the does on the opposite side of the fence. Then he reached back toward his stiffened penis, lifted a hind leg, and shot urine into his mouth. Urine dripped down his beard, and he turned and stared at Mary Beth.

"Charming," she said.

Goliath curled his upper lip, a response to something arousing in the air (biologists call the gesture the "flehmen reaction"). Mary Beth inched closer. They studied each other—woman and buck. Goliath nickered and stamped a front hoof. Mary Beth lunged and grabbed his collar. Goliath bucked. She yanked him down and threw him against the fence. Dona ran to help. He tried to jerk free, but Mary Beth wedged him with her hip against the fence.

"What's the matter, Goliath?" Mary Beth crooned. "You used to like me." His eyes were popping now. His penis hung like a surgical tube. It started to grow stiff again.

"Looks like he's liking you just fine," Dona observed.

"He'll take whatever action he can get," Mary Beth said, and asked for the rag.

I pulled the washcloth from my pocket and handed it to Mary Beth. She rubbed it all over Goliath's soaking beard and down his chest and up along his oily withers. He didn't seem to mind the attention. Mary Beth gave the cloth another good rub along the scent glands on Goliath's head, then held the soiled cloth out to me. I took it between two fingers and dropped it in the coffee can. That was our "buck cloth." The billy rag, the teaser in a can. We'd let the does sniff it when we suspected they were in heat, and if they showed interest in the odor—they were.

Mary Beth released Goliath and he shot away and paced along the fence. The does watched from the opposite side of the wire. Goliath nickered and tongued the air. Unable to reach them, he stretched his head again toward his genitals and slipped his penis into his mouth. Mary Beth looked on with amused patience; she saw this all the time. Goliath removed his organ from his lips and squirted semen into the air and onto his front legs.

"So like a man," Mary Beth observed.

Dona folded her arms and said, "If only they *could*."

The expression "horny" may or may not have come from male goats, but the Italian *mano cornuta,* the horn gesture—the sign for a cuckold—certainly did. In several Mediterranean pastoral cultures male goats were historically thought of as louche and immoral because it was said that they allowed other, less-dominant males to mate with females in their herd. Male sheep, on the other hand, maintain harems, and a ram doesn't tolerate the presence of another ram in his flock. Rams—and ewes by extension—came to be thought of as honorable whereas goat bucks and does were considered dissolute. This may have been the reason why the early Hebrews sacrificed goats as "sin offerings" to appease their god when they'd sinned, and why they sacrificed sheep for celebrations. It may also explain why goats became scapegoats—the ones driven out into the wilderness to atone for men's sins—and why sheep never became scapesheep.

The perceived debauchery of male goats found its most enduring expression in the Greek god Pan. Pan, the goat god—half man, half goat—protected flocks and played the panpipe. He's immortalized in paintings, sculpture, and poetry as the lecherous, avuncular horned god who chased nymphs and drank booze and generally caused mayhem. Pan pursued the nymph Syrinx, who, at his embrace, turned into a reed (from which he made his pipe). He copulated with the Maenads—and there were dozens—*all at once.* His name derived from the Greek *Pa-on* (the grazer) but became in time conflated with the Greek word *Pan,* meaning "All"; thus since antiquity he represented both a roguish horned god and a mystical deity who embodied *all* things—body, mind, spirit; beast, human, god—an original Trinity.

To Ralph Waldo Emerson, the goat god was the "Soul of All Things." To Keats he was the "dread opener of the mysterious doors leading to universal knowledge." To Coleridge, intelligence blended "with a darker power . . . more universal than the conscious intellect of man." People feared Pan partly because of his sexual appetite. He *literally* embraced all (men, women, boys, animals). He was said to strike terror so often that our word *panic* comes from his name—the fright induced by Pan. He, and all goats by extension, became in time associated with the Hebrew *Se'irim*—the satyrs—and their leader, Azazel. Christ used the familiar pastoral imagery when he preached his parable of the good sheep inheriting the heavenly kingdom, and the goats condemned to hell—*and he shall set the sheep on his right hand, but the goats on the left.* Christ's gospel further reinforced the (now) Christian notion of good sheep (lamb of god) and evil goats (satyrs).

Of all the Greek gods, Pan alone is said to have died. He perished, not surprisingly, right after Christ's birth. In time, the god of the old religion became the devil of the new, hoof, horn, tail, and genitals intact. When people today say—and they do so all the time—that goats somehow remind them of the devil, it's the collective mythology they're reminded of, and not necessarily an actual goat.

Goliath stood now against the fence, his head low and penis flaccid. Frustrated and high on hormones, he reared and crashed against his gate. If he couldn't have the females, at least he wanted another male to spar with, horn to horn. But he had no other buck to fight with, and his horns had been burned away soon after birth. Still—his hoofs, his hair, his coat shined in the dull morning air and his amber eyes flared up at us. In a few weeks, Mary Beth would let him run with the female herd and then he'd have orgasm after orgasm all day long with as many does who'd let him. For now all Goliath could do was let off his lightning against a fence.

Service

THE DAY BEFORE THANKSGIVING, HANNAH WENT INTO heat. Her vulva swelled conch-shell pink. She paced the fence line and moaned. When I let her smell the buck cloth in the can late that afternoon, her tail flicked excitedly back and forth. In the sharp chilly sunlight, I saw what we'd been waiting for all month: a string of translucent fluid oozed from her vagina. It looked like donut glaze.

Since we couldn't breed Hannah or Lizzie to Goliath—he was too closely related—we'd found another Nubian herd in New York State. Dottie Cross lived nearly an hour away, and she raised several registered Nubian sires. That afternoon we called and told her we were on our way. By the time we prepared the Saab and got Hannah into the hatch, the day was already fading over Bennetts Ridge. We had little time to lose.

We drove through hills in cold November light. Fires burned on lawns along the way. Hannah wouldn't lie down in the back, but surfed on all fours. Her head bumped the roof, her tailbone the glass of the hatch.

Dottie Cross's ranch house lay beneath a canopy of pines. Doe pens lined the backyard fence, the buck pens near the driveway. Dottie bustled out of the house, a small, cheerful woman in glasses and black gum boots. She'd raised ribbon-winning dairy goats for over thirty years and made goat milk soap. Nearly all her bucks and does had biblical names.

We opened the doors of the Saab, and the bucks in their pens sniffed the air and scrambled toward the fence. Dottie took Hannah's registration papers and studied her dam and sire sides. She knew the lineage of all the Nubians in the area, and was trying to find for her the best match. Meanwhile Hannah at last lay comfortably in the nest of hay in the back of the car. She raised her nose to the air, but wouldn't budge. Three bucks scrummed along the fence and sniffed at the car. *Someone* apparently was throwing heat. I tried to lure Hannah out with some raisins, to no avail. Finally Dona and I muscled her up and threaded a pony strap through her collar. The golden doe stepped down to the pavement, and the bucks sprang to life.

Dona held Hannah tightly by the strap, while Dottie walked around her. Dottie inspected the goat like a car salesman assessing the new floor model. Hannah gave a cautious glance toward the bucks. They were leaping against the fence, hooting and nickering. Dottie looked closer at Hannah's vulva and announced: "This is a doe in standing heat."

By now twilight hung in the branches and our breath made magenta clouds in the cold. The bucks licked the air and tried to get a taste of Hannah's heat. They leered like old men in a strip club, penises erect. A spotted miniature Nubian pushed off the fence and leaped onto the back of a young black purebred and dry-humped him. The larger purebred shook him off with ease, then went behind and dry-humped *him*.

Hannah stood on the pavement flicking her tail. She didn't seem particularly impressed by all the fuss, but her tail decidedly said *Yes!* She hunched her back and let out a stream of hot urine, and the bucks grew more aroused. Their eyes bugged. An aging buck in the neighboring pen circled and moaned.

Dottie decided on Sonny, the black purebred who'd been humping the mini. His coat was India ink and he sported a white topknot, a large Roman nose, and a luxurious black goatee. Winterplace Joyful Sonata was his registered name—Sonny for short.

"You're going to have to help me," Dottie explained. "What we want to do is get Sonny out here without letting the mini out."

"Right," I said.

"You'll have to hold the mini or try to distract him."

"Okay," I said, and approached the fence and tried to distract the mini. I did a little scrimmage dance but the goat ignored me. Both he and Sonny stood side-by-side licking the air. I waved hands in the mini's face. I shouted: *Mini-mini-mini!* Nothing worked. He leered as before.

"The distracting's not working," I said.

Dottie smiled knowingly.

"Plan B," I muttered, and walked up to the fence and stood face-to-face with the mini. He was ripe. He was oily. He was hardly mini—on his back legs he stood as tall as I. I grabbed his sticky collar and held him to the fence and yelled, "Okay." Dottie released the gate and Sonny shot out.

He flew to Hannah's rear. He slurped at her vulva with an acrobatic tongue. Dona held Hannah by the strap while she danced a bit but endured. Sonny licked her flanks. He tasted her vagina again, then turned and sniffed his own risen penis. Hannah was a large goat but next to Sonny she looked petite. When he bulled his enormous head into her behind, her rear legs flew completely off the ground.

Finally he mounted her, his tongue stuck out the side of his mouth. He slipped off, nickered, and mounted again. He looked like he'd flatten her with his weight.

Before it began it was over. Sonny slid off, his half-mast penis dripping semen.

"You have to watch his head," Dottie explained. "You can't look down there. When he tosses his head back, that's when you know"—she picked her words carefully—"they've mated."

Sonny licked Hannah's neck again.

"Kind of romantic," I mused.

Dona gave me a look. Sonny turned and sniffed his penis, then shot urine into his mouth.

"Uh-hmm," Dona said. "*Romantic.*"

As if on cue, Hannah urinated also, and Sonny leaned in and lapped her urine, let it splash down his face and beard. Now Dottie rolled her eyes.

"I'll never get used to this part," she confessed.

The other bucks were pacing their pens while they watched the action. They made a high haunting sound, a back-of-the-throat staccato, the sound of sexual arousal—the same rat-tat-tat human boys make when imitating machine-gun fire: *eh-eh-eh-eh-eh.*

Sonny lowered his head and stretched his neck and curled his upper lip—a display biologists call the "low-stretch." Male ungulates make the gesture when courting females. An estrous female understands the body language (which mimics that of a suckling kid). It's the ungulate equivalent of pillow talk: "I'm not a threat: *let's get it on.*"

Sonny rooted between Hannah's legs once more; then he mounted and clasped her waist a second time.

Once again Dottie reminded me patiently about not looking "down there." But I couldn't help myself. I was obsessed with down there. I wanted to see the connection, the contact, the insertion. How else would we know it worked? We were paying customers after all, and the light was falling dimly through the trees. The bucks hooted, the does bleated, Dottie's dog barked from the house. I wanted to catch a glimpse, an assurance of insemination. For in the lingering dusk, under the pines in the encroaching night, it seemed we were all watching some ancient evening theater, a ruminant striptease. Goat porn. Live and close up. Dona wheeled Hannah into position once more. Hannah was growing antsy now. Was the moment lost? She stared into the foliage above her head, the dry oaks, the pines. Was she thinking of those leaves? A postcoital snack? Was she thinking of England? Or—in her case—Nubia? The Aswan Dam?

Sonny mounted her again and again. The fourth time his red needle stiffened and went inside Hannah and he tossed his head back like a bronco—and he was done.

Dottie grabbed his collar and started dragging him back to his lockup. The show was over. Then Sonny broke from her grip and dashed across the lawn. He raced from one enclosure to the next, sniffing and nickering in the twilight. There were other estrous does to mate with and this was his chance. Dottie went after him. I did too. "The he-goat is immoderate in its desires," the Roman agriculturalist Columella wrote in A.D. 70. "While it is still being fed at its mother's udder, it leaps upon her and tries to do her violence. Hence, before it has reached six years of age, it is fast becoming old . . . it has worn itself out in early youth by premature indulgence of its desires."

Sonny was already two and the clock was ticking fast. He wanted more "premature indulgences of desire." I cornered him by a fence, grabbed his urine-soaked collar, and yanked him across the lawn. This time Dottie distracted the mini while I fought Sonny back into his pen. In the end, he seemed almost relieved to go back in. But as soon as the latch closed he sprang to life once more. He reared and crashed down on the mini's head, then shoved his newly fragrant beard into the mini's face. He paraded and strutted. *He seemed to be bragging.* The mini leaped on his back and dry-humped him again. Did I imagine the boasting, the strut? Dottie read my thoughts.

"It's like a frat house," she said with a little embarrassment.

Dona was saying something from the car now. I stood transfixed by the boys. The humping turned to wrestling and back to humping. The old buck in the nearby pen thrashed his fence. Dona finally shouted: "*Are you going to help or just watch?*"

She was trying to load Hannah into the hatch. She and Dottie looked at me with dismay.

I left the brawling bucks, though I didn't want to. I helped trundle Hannah back into the car. She seemed weak and stank of Sonny. Dona gently shut the hatch. I took the driver's seat. Dottie slipped a piece of paper through the passenger window. A "Service Memorandum" from the American Dairy Goat Association. She'd filled out the form in blue pen. Date of service. Owner of the Dam at Time Served. The fee read: $35.

For a long time on the road neither Dona nor I spoke. We watched the night resolve through the windshield, a stab of red cinders in the west. My hands and jeans reeked of buck. Hannah stood in the farthest corner in the back, her head drooping down. She hadn't moved once since getting back into the car.

Dona finally asked, "Is she all right?"

I was wondering the same. Dona held some raisins out to Hannah, who hung her head against the window without interest. Something clearly was going on with the doe; was it confusion, shame, awareness? What could we know of the goat's feelings, her mind, her interior life? Whenever we put sentiments into animals' heads they're usually just our own echoed back. Then it dawned on me—at last—that Hannah was simply worn out. She'd been bulled around and entered four times and hung on repeatedly by a buck twice her size. She was probably just exhausted.

Back in our valley, a platinum moon hung above the house. Frost laid wickerwork across the lawn. All the goats stood outside by the fence as if awaiting Hannah's return. In the paddock, they crowded around her and sniffed her new exciting scent. Lizzie seemed particularly interested in the odor—and in four days hence she'd come into heat and we'd drive her to Dottie's as well.

That night we left the car doors open to air, but Sonny's musk lingered for a long time on the cracked leather seats. We could smell buck on Hannah for weeks, especially after it rained. With any luck, in 150 days, Hannah—and then Lizzie—would deliver one kid goat, or two, or three. *Chad gadya.*

Paradise

THERE'S AN OLD YIDDISH TALE THAT TELLS OF A SICKLY man who bought a dairy goat because his doctor said goat milk would cure his ills. After weeks of drinking the goat's milk, the man was healthy again.

One morning his goat disappeared. The man and his son searched everywhere but the doe couldn't be found. A day later she appeared in their doorway, her udder so full it touched the ground. When the son milked her he found the milk extraordinarily sweet and rich. It tasted like milk and honey.

Soon the doe disappeared again, and again returned with a gravid udder; and this went on for days—the goat leaving home and coming back and the milk always tasting "of paradise." The son grew curious about where she went. So one evening he tied a long tether to her tail and when the tether slipped out the door he followed her into the dusk.

The goat walked through the night. In the morning she came to a cave and went inside. The boy followed the tug of the tether through the dark, and the sound of the doe's hoofs led him on. At last they emerged into daylight, and a lush green land spread before them; fat grapes hung from vines, honey dripped from trees. The boy understood at once: he'd arrived in the land of milk and honey. Through the dark cave the goat had led him to paradise.

The folktale doesn't end well; what Yiddish ones do? Yet what interests me is how a goat led a boy to paradise. How careful attention to one animal took him through a rabbit hole and revealed a hidden world. "Every species of animal," writes E. O. Wilson, "opens the gates to the paradisiacal world." If you follow living beings assiduously in the field, or through the lens of a microscope, they lead you to an understanding of their lives, and *all* life. They usher you into a kind of Eden.

The more I read about goats, the more I kept finding the same theme about goats helping humans or leading them to unexpected places. An Arab legend tells how a goat directed a herder to the coffee bean. He found his goats eating red berries from a bush one day and acting frisky after. He tried the berries himself and discovered coffee. The Greek goat goddess Amalthea fed all mankind by cracking the horn off her head; it became the cornucopia, the horn of plenty, eternally filled with food for mankind. Amalthea nursed Zeus himself, and thus a goat was the foster mother of an entire race of rascally Greek gods—and the Roman ones that followed.

Goats were the first animals humans ever domesticated after the dog. The first nonhuman milk people ever drank came from a goat (the cow entered the picture thousands of years later). Goats were domesticated in the Near East around 10,000 B.C. Unlike gazelles—which Egyptians tried to domesticate—goats were relatively easy to breed in captivity. They were a rugged herbivore who ate a wide-ranging diet and were more or less willing to follow humans. Around 5000 B.C., when migrants from the Near East began moving into southern Europe, they were accompanied by goats. When a second wave of pioneers came from Central Asia, they also came with goats. The DNA indicates that these early goat migrants derived from five distinct maternal lines all originating in the Near East and Central Asia. These five genetic lines were transported first to Europe, and then to the rest of the world. Today's domestic goats retain the same genetic material from the original five lines; they also retain more genetic diversity than any other livestock species. This meant the goats in our backyard—Hannah and Lizzie, Nisa and Pie—were direct descendants of goats who accompanied humans at the beginning of recorded time.

From the start our relationship with the goats felt atavistic. That first fall when we sat with them on Mason's Hill, or walked with them in the woods, their odor of hair and hide seemed oddly familiar. The sound of them cropping leaves, the high tinkle of their bells, their voices calling across the lawn became the music of those autumn afternoons, a music tantalizingly familiar—a song just beyond the reach of an unremembered past.

Labor

THE DAYS GREW SHORT IN DECEMBER AND THE NIGHTS brought squalls of snow. The does retreated increasingly to their barn. One morning they woke to a foot of powder piled on the lawn. Nisa and Pie, the kids, had never seen snow before and they stared out the barn door as if surveying floodwater. Hannah and Lizzie—veterans—plowed into the drifts. The kids followed cautiously behind, lowering and raising heads, trying to get a read on all that white. All four trudged thigh-high and made a luge track around the pasture. They stopped at every spruce along the way; and this became their routine each winter morning, circumambulating the pasture and munching spruce needles, their daily dose of vitamin C.

The new year arrived and the nights turned arctic. We fed the goats hay inside the barn. The dry grass worked like wood inside a furnace. The more roughage they ate, the warmer they grew within—central heating, ruminant style. Goats are notoriously wasteful eaters. The word *capricious* comes from *capra* partially because of the way goats eat. A well-fed goat will pick through hay and reject 20 to 50 percent of it while filling her dietary needs. If a piece of hay (or an apple or sugar cube) falls to the ground, she won't touch it. Despite tales of goats eating "everything," our does were fussy eaters. They wasted almost a quarter of the hay in their mangers. The fallen hay became their bedding, and in winter we let it build up, along with their feces, on the barn floor. All that organic matter made a comfortable mattress that slowly released its heat on frozen nights. When ten below outside, the barn stayed five above.

Each day that winter we fed the does salt and minerals—phosphorus, potassium, cobalt, copper, magnesium, sulfur, iodine, calcium, zinc. The mixture came in forty-pound bags. The salt was essential for their digestion and the minerals kept them healthy. They lapped the powdered elements from our hands as if they were sugar.

By Valentine's Day, Hannah and Lizzie began to show a bulge in their starboard sides. In March they grew enormous. While Pie and Nisa ran circles around them in the melting snow, the pregnant sisters waddled. They grew ravenous and fought over choice bits of hay, and chased the kids away from the mangers to eat all by themselves. In the first three months inside the womb, the fetus of a kid develops slowly. Most of the big growth occurs in the last two months of the doe's pregnancy. Heretofore we'd been feeding Hannah and Lizzie exclusively hay, but by March we gave them each a pan of grain—oats, corn, and wheat coated in cane molasses. They needed the extra protein in their late pregnancy, to build up reserves for their coming lactation.

Some days that March rose into the fifties and the pregnant sisters lay side-by-side in pale sunshine and groaned. Bluebirds appeared on warm days and searched for nesting sites. The goats rubbed themselves against the fencing and teased out tufts of winter hair. They shed their heavy coats throughout the month. The welded wire fence turned into a wall of carded wool. Sparrows stole the hairs to line their nests.

We didn't know that spring how many kids were growing inside Hannah or Lizzie. Goats tend to birth twins, but they can also throw singletons, triplets, and quadruplets (even quintuplets). Those April nights I studied the birthing pages of the goat books: *Storey's Guide to Raising Dairy Goats,* Mackenzie's *Goat Husbandry,* Smith and Sherman's *Goat Medicine*. By mid-April we started gathering kidding supplies: rags, towels, a bottle of 7 percent iodine. We bought a bottle of selenium and vitamin E mixture, with which to inject the newborns (without it they can develop white muscle disease); 20-gauge needles and syringes; baby bottles and plastic nipples (to feed the newborns with); a box of surgical gloves and a tube of KY jelly. If the does had difficulty during labor and a kid was stuck in the birth canal—or twins got their legs entangled there—one of us would have to go into the uterus with a gloved hand and help pull the fetus out.

All the gear was ready, but were we? Dona had helped deliver several human babies before—she was a trained doula—but she'd never delivered a goat. I had no experience at all, and *Goat Medicine,* the vet manual, lent me little confidence. Each page warned of another dire possibility, a breech birth, a retained placenta, pregnancy toxemia. Stillborns. Three whole pages alone were devoted to "abnormal fetal presentation": upside-down kids, backward kids, heads or forelegs back, twisted-up twins, triplets stacked side-by-side like slices of Wonder Bread across the birth canal, and no way to get them out. Mary Beth Bolduc said she'd help in a pinch, but she lived almost an hour away. In all likelihood, the goats would birth with no problems. Yet the real reason we needed to be around at birth was difficult to explain, even to myself at the time. It struck at the heart of the husbandry we were going to practice and came down to this simple question: How does a human and not the intended kid or calf obtain milk from a lactating animal? The answer: By coercion and deceit. We needed to be around at birth to enact an age-old sleight of hand.

Mid-April, grass inched out of the earth again. The wild leeks erupted along the brook. On the afternoon of April 26, Hannah stayed in the barn while the others went out to graze. A small discharge of cloudy fluid hung from her vulva. I checked the ligaments that attached her tail to the pinbone near the base of her spine. During the day the ligaments had softened considerably, and now I could place my palms on either side of her tail where it met her spine, and press the flesh there close together—a sure sign she would kid sometime in the next twelve hours.

Kidding occurs in three stages. First, uterine contractions force the placenta and fetus against the cervix and dilate it. Then the doe begins to strain and have contractions and eventually delivers her kid (or kids). Lastly the doe expels her placenta. Hannah was already in the first stage. The kid—or kids—were being forced up against her cervix, and we could see the hollowing in her flanks now that the fetus was moving toward her rump. We cleaned the barn, laid down fresh hay. Hannah could kid anytime in the night or early next morning. All we could do was wait.

At dusk a smoky light hung in the spruces and the air smelled of plowed earth. Pie and Nisa and Lizzie returned from the pasture, but Hannah blocked the entrance to the barn. When the others tried to go in, Hannah's hackles rose and she fought them off one by one. She wanted the barn to herself to kid; and we wished our barn was bigger or had a kidding stall. After a few minutes, Hannah stepped resignedly inside and let the others drift in behind.

At nine o'clock all the goats bedded down for the night. Hannah sat by herself in a corner. At ten she was up and pacing. At eleven she chewed her cud. At midnight I gave up; she rested now alongside Lizzie. Perhaps nothing would happen in the night.

I went upstairs to bed, set the alarm for two, and listened out the window one last time. All was silent save the brook; I joined Dona in bed and fell to sleep.

At one a.m. a blue moon glared through the panes. I drifted in and out of sleep and woke with a start. Lola was pacing beside the window; she must have heard something in the night. I shook Dona awake. The clock read 1:52.

Outside the night lay cold and starless. The goats stood in the paddock under the moon. In the barn Hannah stood alone beneath a yellow lightbulb, ears out to the side 747 style. A red water balloon the size of a pomegranate pouched from her vulva. She gave me an uncertain look, then opened her mouth wide in a yawn. The rest of the herd was just hoofing toward the back swing door. I leaped the gate and locked the door to keep them out. Hannah would have the barn to herself after all.

Now that it was dark and cold and the middle of the night everything I'd read in the past few weeks flew instantly out of my head. What was the pomegranate hanging from her vulva? Her amniotic fluid? Her afterbirth? The bag was all ruby brilliance, filled with what looked like Jell-O. Why no hoofs, no legs, no kid? Lola was barking madly across the lawn. The goats moaned and bumped against the locked door. Dona flew inside wearing a denim coat, tying back her hair. She took one look at the bag and assured me: her water. Everything was fine.

She came in through the gate and squatted beside Hannah and talked to her. The golden doe knelt now on her forelegs, her rear up in the air. Then her eyes rolled back in their sockets and her body began to ripple. She huffed and blew air out her nostrils. The water bag sucked in and out of her vulva, and then the contractions passed. The bag had made no progress.

In a normal birth a kid's front hoofs emerge first from the vulva, and nestled right on top of the legs comes the kid's nose. Its head and body are presented in a streamlined position, the kid arriving in the world in a forward dive. Any other position may present problems, and so far no hoofs were in sight. We weren't sure how long Hannah had been in active labor, but knew that if nothing emerged within thirty minutes—no hoofs or tail or nose—we'd have to glove up and investigate inside her uterus.

Hannah's contractions began again. Her body undulated. The water bag sucked in and out, then ceased. Once again the bag made no visible progress.

Of all the possible kidding scenarios in the veterinary manual, the one that stuck in mind that night was this: the kid's head emerges first from his mother's vulva, but his misaligned backward legs get caught in the birth canal; and in the ensuing struggle to push him out, his jugular vein is pinched so tight he chokes to death before he's even born. The problem then is trying to save the doe.

Hannah leaned into a sit, then plopped onto her side and rested her head against the wall. She looked at Dona and moaned. Then she lay completely on her side in hay, her newly swollen teats pointing in the air. She looked exhausted already. Her tongue lolled from her mouth. Dona pulled a sugar cube from her coat pocket. Hannah gobbled it and right away started pushing. She curled her upper lip; stretched her legs. Now it seemed the golden doe knew what to do. Hannah pushed and grunted and a second bag emerged beside the first, this one clear and glaucous. Her contractions ceased and she searched for yet more sugar.

"Good girl, Hannah," Dona said and handed her another cube.

Something was sticking out of Hannah's vulva now, a black stub with white in the center: a tiny hoof.

Hannah blew air out of her nostrils, then pushed again. Now the hoof and leg emerged clearly; and a second hoof dropped too. Two legs inched out—black, velvety, crossed delicately over each other.

"Good Hannah," Dona kept saying. "Good girl."

A black bump appeared nestled on top of the legs. Two nostrils. The nose. A pink tongue. Hannah was screaming now in a low baritone. Out slid the kid's nose and mouth in painfully slow motion while Hannah blew and yelled. The nose and mouth alone were enormous. How would it ever pass through her vulva? Hannah's eyes widened; she let out a shocking scream. The water bag broke and the kid's head slipped out and dangled in the air in a jelly of clear mucus. With one last heave, Hannah screamed again and pushed out the rest of the kid: out spilled water and blood and amniotic fluid. The kid flopped on the floor like a landed fish.

"*Good Hannah!*" Dona said with excitement.

Hannah stretched her neck back to inspect her baby. Dona cleared the warm web of mucus from the kid's mouth as it gasped for air. Hannah gave her kid a tentative lick, then she addressed her newborn in a tender pleading tone—a voice she'd never used before. The kid was black with a pile of white on its head and long white ears. Hannah licked it vigorously about the face, then turned and opened her mouth wide and yawned—the flehmen response—and returned to licking her baby. Dona turned the kid over: she was a doeling—a girl—her fur sopping wet, her eyes slate gray; little brown stripes ran down her face.

Hannah rose slowly and stood on shaky legs. She rested for a moment while strings of fluid leaked from her behind. She still looked large; we thought at least one more kid might lie inside. She stepped to the corner beside the manger and lowered her head once more.

The second kid came quickly. Hannah delivered standing and the kid swam out of her, backflipped in the air, and plopped upside down on the floor. Hannah licked the new kid's face, yawned, and licked again. This one was copper—the color of a new penny. A doeling too. She dog-paddled in the lagoon of her marine birth as if trying to reach dry land. I helped free her front and back legs from the caul of warm mucus. Hannah talked to her in her plaintive maternal voice. Meanwhile the black kid was already staggering around on wobbly legs. Hannah went to the water bucket and took a long suck of water. Another red sack now hung from her rear. She drank for a full thirty seconds, then looked up, water dripping from her beard. We weren't sure if she was done or if a third kid lay inside, but she looked hollow now, her stomach half the size it had been before. Her contractions had stopped, but she hadn't passed her placenta yet. That would tell us she was done and out of danger.

We toweled off the doelings. Each weighed about seven

pounds. Their umbilical cords had broken during birth, and hung like wet gray noodles, five inches long. Dona held one doeling in her lap while I snipped the dangling umbilicus with scissors. I poured iodine into a 35 mm film canister and bathed the cut end of the umbilicus to prevent infection. Hannah stood by the water bucket watching the bipeds minister to her babies. Dona toweled off the kids some more. Their long white ears were damp and folded lengthwise, sealed like envelopes. We peeled each ear open as if they were unread letters.

The kids were getting hungry now. They stumbled around the floor searching for a warm teat. Yet the moment the older one drew close to her mother, we picked her up and placed her back on a towel. We weren't going to let them suckle off Hannah. The human trickery had already begun. It was time to milk the goat.

Milk evolved 300 million years ago along with the advent of hair and warm-bloodedness and skin glands—all of which distinguish mammals from other species. Milk gave mammalian mothers a perfect diet with which to feed their newborns. It gave mammals as a whole a tremendous advantage over other classes of animals, and allowed them to conquer every corner of the earth and sea.

The word *mammal* comes from the Latin *mammalis,* "of the breast." The first food a mammal tastes is breast milk. They drink their mother's milk only in infancy. Humans are the only mammals who've effectively prolonged their infancy by continuing to drink milk long into adulthood. They do this by exploiting the breasts of other mammals—namely those with hoofs. Eleven thousand years ago, during the early Neolithic, humans learned that instead of killing a lactating gazelle or ibex or bezoar goat for meat, they could keep the animal penned and steal her milk. Since milk is the liquid that bonds child and mother, these early pastoralists discovered that if they pilfered the milk, they also controlled the offspring. Milk, they learned, was power.

Most dairies today consider the whole messy business of breeding—the insemination, pregnancy, birthing, and baby animal itself—a necessary evil to get what they want: milk. Nearly all dairies large and small (organic or not) practice a form of apartheid between mother and child. The moment the calf or kid or lamb is born—or a day or a week later—the baby is plucked from the birthing stall or field and put on a bottle, and the mother is sent to be milked. The happy calf suckling its dam may be our storybook image of pastoralism, but it almost never happens in a commercial operation. Every dairy we knew—cow or goat—pulled its calves or kids from their mothers right away or a few days after birth. We decided to do the same with our kids. We'd milk the mothers and dole the liquid to the newborns. In this way we'd imprint ourselves on the kids and they'd be tame and friendly and not afraid of humans. We'd be all things to all the goats: mother, kid, milker, herd king and queen.

A few weeks earlier I'd bought some baby bottles at a drugstore. Mary Beth Bolduc had given us a clear plastic nipple that worked for newborn kids. At the store I showed the nipple to the elderly saleswoman at the counter.

"Nuks," she announced smilingly and showed me to their shelf.

Back at the register she rang up eight bottles and eight plastic nipples. She asked if I was expecting twins.

Yes, I said distractedly, two pairs. Maybe even some triplets.

Her smile froze. I tried to explain—*goats*—but it was too late to recover. I took my nipples and scurried out the door.

Now I carried the Nuks and bottles in a basket through the gate in the barn. The bottles were plastic Gerbers—four- and eight-ounce—with screw bands in nursery blues and pinks. Dona was going to milk Hannah for the first time, yet it seemed just then to make more sense to simply let the newborns suckle off their mother. Already the black doeling was crawling perilously close to Hannah's warm teats; and each time she drew near, we plucked her away, but within seconds she'd motor back like a wind-up toy. How cruel it seemed to deny the kid her first desire in life: milk from her mother's teat. Yet if we let the kids suckle off their mothers, they'd be attached forever and we'd never get them off the teat, never know how much each kid was drinking, and couldn't control them in the future. If we wanted clean milk, and tame and friendly goats, this was how the husbandry was done. Hannah had been bottle-raised, and Lizzie and Pie and Nisa. None were allowed to suckle off their mother. None of them were what Mary Beth Bolduc called "mother suckers." "Kid off the dam," she'd told us, "or a damned kid." The newborns cried. Hannah called for them to nurse. We kept them back. At last I understood the true meaning of the word *kidnapping.*

Dona left and returned with a milk pail and a wooden stool. The smell of the April morning blew briefly through the door. Lola came in and wagged her tail at the newborns and sniffed them through the gate. I hung a square plastic bucket over a crossbeam at the height of Hannah's nose and filled it with a scoop of grain. Dona set the low stool on the floor of the barn. Normally Hannah was ravenous, but now she investigated her oats, took a few nibbles, and looked back at her babies. She called to them and ate a bite more. Dona sat on the stool beside her and reached under her belly and squeezed faint squirts of milk from her teats—a thin hiss on stainless steel. We couldn't afford to lose any of Hannah's first milk. Her colostrum, like human colostrum, was full of immunoglobulins, vitamins, and growth hormones. Her first milk came thick and yellow like clotted cream. "Beestings," the English call the colostrum, or "beastmilk." So rich and creamy, a scant cup can replace two eggs in a custard.

Dona finished milking. I brought over a flake of our best hay and a handful of raisins for Hannah. Dona took the milk pail to the table on the other side of the gate, poured colostrum into two baby bottles, and saved the rest for later feedings. The new twins lay sleeping now on a blanket. Their velvet coats were damp but nearly dry. The copper kid woke and made little squeaking sounds. The black one let out a startling hunger cry—*maaaa!*

Dona picked up the black doeling. I took the copper one. Each of us held a four-ounce plastic bottle. The black kid caught on right away and began sucking greedily at the plastic Nuk. My copper one kept missing, spastically mouthing the plastic and not latching on. Hannah picked at her oats. She came over from time to time to watch and nicker or lick one of her babies on the head. The copper kid was still having trouble. I held her head up and forced the nipple into her mouth, and soon she latched on too and started sucking. Each polished off three ounces of their mother's milk. Afterward, we put them on the floor and they staggered around like street junkies, drunk on colostrum. The plastic Nuks were now their friend.

Before they fell asleep again, I went outside the gate, pulled up two syringes of selenium and vitamin E—one cc each.

Dona held the doelings in her arms while I pinched the little flesh around their shoulders and slipped the sharps beneath their skin. Each kid wailed when the needle went in—ear-splittingly loud.

It was nearing four a.m. by now. Outside the night was turning over and the new day smelled of onion grass and loam; sunrise wouldn't be long. We cleaned the barn. We shoveled wet piles of amniotic fluid. Blood. Placenta. Manure. Urine-soaked hay. Lola stood staring at the newborns through the gate. We let the rest of the herd inside and they crowded around the new twins and sniffed them and sniffed Hannah. Then we set the twins inside a dog crate lined with hay on the other side of the gate, near enough so Hannah could see and smell them. Finally I went outside to stretch.

There were nights when we used to live in New York City when I stayed awake until dawn while Dona helped deliver a friend's child. Weary mornings of postpartum stories, celebration. The thrilling door that opened each time an infant was born, as if all the air had suddenly been freshened inside a room. It felt a tiny bit that way that April morning with the night fading overhead—excitement laced with worry; not as big or life-changing, infinitesimal by comparison. But a birth is a birth nonetheless.

Sometime that morning before the sun rose, I asked Dona how it was different, delivering a goat instead of a human. She was cleaning afterbirth, tossing soiled towels out of the barn. She stopped and thought a moment, then went back to tossing towels.

"Someone else," she said, "cleans up after."

PART II

Milk

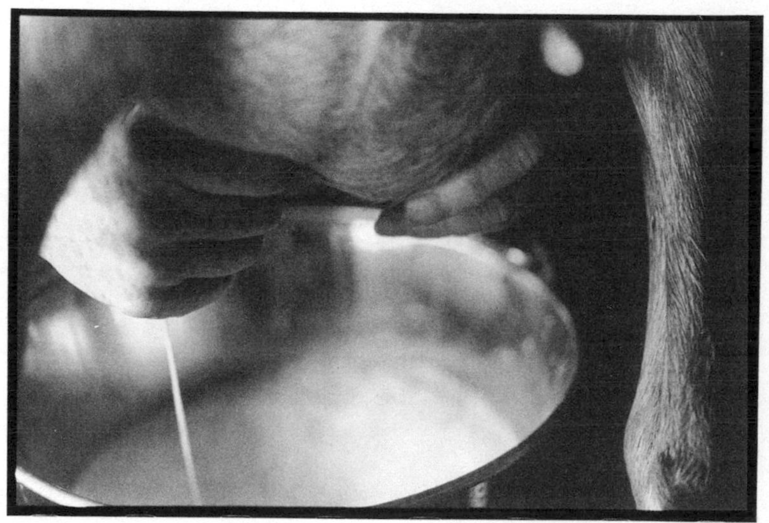

Culture

THE SENTENCE YOU ARE READING RIGHT NOW CONTAINS at least nineteen hidden references to pastoralism. It does so through the letters *A, C, H, L,* and *I*—all of which retain in their shape their pictographic origin, resembling either a hoofed animal or a tool used to herd it.

The Roman letter *A* comes from the Hebrew aleph, derived from the word for "ox." The animal's head appears when the letter is turned upside down—∀—its two horns sticking up to heaven. The Roman *C* comes from the Hebrew gimel, for "camel." Tip the *C* on its side and the camel's hump rears into view: ∩. *H,* from the Hebrew heth, is an enclosure or fence. Our *H* retains the two posts and crossbar of a fence; enlarged and strung together the letters could keep animals penned in: **HHHHHH**. *L* is the Hebrew lamed, a shepherd's staff or cattle prod. *I* is another type of staff, from the Hebrew waw, for "cane." Both letters writ large—**I** or **L**—would make stout herding sticks.

The point of this pedantry is to show how in our daily life we encounter bits of our cultural past as herders. Every time we scan the alphabet we touch a piece of pastoralism. We're reminded, however unconsciously, that we once lived among, and depended upon, hoofed animals. They were not only our food, but also our vehicles, clothing, tractors, tents, dynamos, vessels, and musical instruments. They helped build our cities and grind our grain and carry our water. Their bodies formed the basis of so much of our early culture. Their skins became our first books.

Homo sapiens evolved as a species thinking, hunting, watching, and eating ungulates: bison and horses, ibex, aurochs, and deer. Our big brains, our wolf-pack sociability, our gamesmanship evolved in concert with hunting large hoofed animals. Our earliest representational art—paintings from the Paleolithic era found in caves from Spain to Africa, Australia to India—shows a singular obsession with herbivores. Animals were humans' first intellectual and aesthetic preoccupation. They figured among our first gods and goddesses. We drew them and dreamed them, sang them and ate them; and our passion for hoofed beings only deepened once we herded instead of hunted them.

Some of the oldest found writing in the world comes from Uruk in southern Mesopotamia and dates to the fourth millennium B.C. The writings were etched with reeds on wet clay tablets and the tablets left to bake in the sun. The very first written records from Uruk are tallies of grazing animals entrusted to specific herdsmen by their owners. It's intriguing that the earliest known writing concerned itself with herding; and equally intriguing are poems found in nearby Sumer a thousand years later—hymns to Sumerian gods and goddesses filled with pastoral imagery. One fragment from 2000 B.C. describes Geshtinanna (the sister of the Sumerian shepherd god, Dammuzi). The poem blends so clearly the later oft-linked worlds of pastoralism and song.

His sister of the sweet-voiced lyre,
Maid Geshtinanna, sits in the fold,
She milks the ewe and gives to the lamb,
She milks the goat and gives to the kid,
In her right hand she carries the churn,
In her left the young woman has a lyre and a harp.

Pastoralism is a way of life based on breeding and herding domestic ungulates: cows, horses, goats, sheep, llamas, vicuñas, reindeer, camels, and yaks, to list a few. Pastoralism first appeared in the Near East and Central Asia in the Neolithic Era—about ten thousand years ago. What started as a new food economy became in time an institution with its own values, rituals, and social powers. Once humans relied on hoofed animals for their livelihood, their view of the world began to change. The first pastoralists developed a different cosmology from that of the hunters and gatherers who preceded them. To hunting cultures animals were equals, independent, numinous. They appeared and disappeared at will. Domesticated animals, on the other hand, had no such autonomy or power or independence. They were not a gift of a god—or a god itself—but were instead beasts bred by and for humans. As such, they could be used, misused, traded, or killed at will. They were, in short, commodities. Goats, sheep, horses, cows, and bulls became wealth.

Friedrich Engels argued that the domestication of cattle was a pivotal point for human society. Once the wild bull was broken and used to plow fields he could also be used for trade. Some humans inevitably accumulated more cattle wealth than others. The spread of a pastoralist economy, Engels implied, led to a growing inequality between those who had and those who hadn't—between rich and poor, and men and women. The end result was a new class system. The contemporary archaeologist David W. Anthony lends fuel to Engels's theory. Anthony observed that when people started keeping domestic sheep and cattle on the Eurasian steppes, around 5000 B.C., a society of chieftains appeared where none had existed before. The chieftains distinguished themselves from the "common people" through ostentatious funerals, elaborate jewelry, and animal sacrifice—practices unknown to those who still foraged and didn't accept the new animal currency. The cultural rift between foragers and pastoralists grew. The chieftains on the Eurasian steppes accumulated more and more animals—and more power and land. The foragers did not. The chieftains and their herding culture survived and spread. The foraging cultures diminished and died out.

In time herding cultures took over most parts of the globe. Migrants came with their hoofed animals to new lands, or rode them there. Pastoralist empires conquered the world. The Persian, Roman, Mongol, Mughal, British, and Spanish sent their armies across the earth. With them came their domestic cattle, sheep, horses, and goats—and a different way of thinking than the natives. They spread their herders' diet, heavy with butter and milk, meat and cheese, and their economy, based on animal wealth. Hunters, gatherers, and foragers had to make way for the new culture and economy, as they've been making way in the tundras and rainforests of the world until this day.

The first money pastoralist cultures struck was conceived in terms of the market value of hoofed animals. In the Near East, sixty shekels equaled one *manu,* the amount carried by a donkey. Twenty shekels equaled an ox; a goat was worth five. The coins themselves often featured figures of their beloved bulls or rams. The word *pecuniary* ("relating to money") came from the word for "cattle"—*pecus*—in ancient Rome. The original stock market involved itself with *live* stock, the wealth of herded animals. The fetishism of capital came from a living place. Before money talked, it walked.

The longer I lived with goats the more I began to understand the herder's obsession with his animals, his delight in watching them, the way they formed not only his wealth and diet but his frame of reference and metaphoric reach. The twentieth-century social anthropologist E. E. Evans-Pritchard lamented his subjects' monomania with their cattle. "They are always talking about their beasts," he complained of the southern Sudanese Nuer. "I used to sometimes despair that I never discussed anything with the young men but livestock and girls, and even the subject of girls led inevitably to that of cattle. Start on whatever subject I would . . . we would soon be speaking of cows and oxen, heifers and steers, rams and sheep . . . their social idiom is a bovine idiom."

How much is our own idiom in the West, particularly in North America, a "bovine idiom" if not a pastoralist one? How much is our fast food, our market, our poems, our lush green lawns—our cowboy culture—a consequence of a pastoralist past? My *American Heritage Dictionary of the English Language* defines *culture* primarily as "the cultivation of the soil" and secondarily as "the breeding of animals" and thirdly as the "growing of micro-organisms in a medium." Only by the fourth and fifth definitions come the meanings we most commonly ascribe to the word *culture* today: "social and intellectual formation . . . behavior patterns, arts, beliefs."

The progressive meaning of the word is revealing, for the mother of our culture is agriculture; all our other arts sprang from it. The ox to pull the plow. The staff to herd him. The fence to hold him in. The cane to keep him there. *Aleph, lamed, heth, waw*. Even our letters spell it out.

Udder

RAIN ARRIVED THE DAY AFTER HANNAH DELIVERED. The newborn twins shivered in the barn. We fed them warmed bottles of colostrum kept from the night before. The kids stood on shaky legs and wagged their tails, sucked the plastic nipples the way they would their mother's teats. Afterward they clomped around the barn floor on new rubber hoofs, leaped and jerked sideways, explored the walls, peed. Hannah sniffed them through the gate and nickered and they each talked back to her. She'd passed her placenta in the night, and now a rope of blood and afterbirth—lochia—hung from her behind. Fluid would keep dripping from her for days.

Our milk stand was a two-by-four-foot iron platform with an upright stanchion on one side, like the frame of a guillotine. The doe would stick her head through the frame to get to a hanging grain bucket, and a pivoted slat would lock her head in place. Hannah leaped up to the stand that first morning and devoured her grain. Dona sat and milked her from the side. A freezing rain blew against the barn. Hannah munched grain while Dona milked, squirt by squirt. Hannah's milk was still colored with colostrum, but not as thick or yellow as the night before. Afterward, Hannah went back through the gate without a fuss.

The rain turned to wet snow later that morning. We fed the newborns four ounces of Hannah's milk throughout the day. We milked again in the cold that evening. The kids had their last feed before dark. Everything so far had gone without a hitch.

The next morning the sky cleared and Hannah stood alone beside the fence in the coral dawn. A mist hung over the valley, and the brief snow had disappeared. When Hannah spied me in the bedroom window, she let out a harrowing shriek—louder and longer than ever before. I pulled on jeans and went downstairs to see what was wrong; I grabbed the milk pail on the way out to the barn. All the goats now stood in morning light. Hannah paced and screamed. Her udder had grown enormous overnight and hung like a basketball between her legs.

I let her out of the gate in the barn and she leaped up to the milk stand and started eating grain. Yet when I went to milk her, she scraped my hands away with her hind foot. I touched her teats again, squeezed a few squirts into the pail, but every few seconds, she lifted her leg to knock my hands away. I'd milked our neighbor's goats before and had gotten the knack for how it was done; yet I was new to milking—and Hannah was too. I squeezed her teats, and again had to block her kicking feet. She finished her grain, backed up, and kicked more violently than before. My arms began to cramp; I broke into a sweat. Hannah slammed the pail with her foot. Milk flew everywhere—and the pail crashed to the floor.

Dona appeared in the doorway. The newborns were crying now in their crate. I picked up the dripping pail and handed it over—Dona was the more experienced milker. Calmly, she bunched her hair, filled Hannah's grain bucket, and sat to milk the goat. Yet the moment she touched Hannah's teat, Hannah bucked again. Something apparently had happened overnight, and Hannah now wouldn't let herself be milked; she gave Dona the same treatment. Finally I had to grab Hannah's rear legs and hold them down while Dona tried to milk her out.

Every goat breeder has a story of a problem milker, a doe who kicks or fusses on the stand or doesn't allow herself to be milked out. The solution in most dairies is to get rid of the goat. We didn't know back then that Hannah, our first milker, was just such a difficult doe; though we knew from that morning on that milking her was a Herculean task. The next few days, the moment Hannah's head locked into the stand and one of us touched her teats, she danced and kicked. She found the milk pail beneath her and punted it onto the floor. Sometimes in the middle of milking she just lifted her hind foot—soiled with manure—and dipped it delicately in the pail as if it were a footbath. We milked her twice a day, morning and evening, and tried everything. Dona milked. I milked. We milked her from one side and the other, sitting facing her rear, sitting facing her front. Dona tried the Norwegian method of standing and straddling the doe backward and leaning over in a forward bend, head to one side, arms hanging down to milk. It didn't work. I attempted the Mexican technique of sitting astride the goat and wrapping one leg around her hind leg in a leg lock. No go. Equally disconcerting was the way Hannah carried on those first few days. She'd stand on the hill in sunshine and bellow like a car alarm. When I went out to see what was wrong, she'd quiet down. She'd whimper and moan in her plaintive maternal voice and slather my face with her tongue. Yet the moment I left the paddock, she'd start screaming again. Did pulling her kids right after their birth create this mess? Had Hannah bonded with *me* the night of her delivery? Was that why she called to the house as if calling her kids to suckle? No, Mary Beth assured us. She was just a new milker, a first-time freshener; she'd settle down in a day or two; the screaming was normal, she said. The first week was always rough for a young mother.

Afternoons proved worse. Around two o'clock Hannah's udder grew frighteningly large. It looked as if someone had blown up a Mickey Mouse balloon and pinned it upside down between her back legs. She waddled around with that enormous bag and screamed. *Kid off the dam or a damned kid.* The kids weren't damned but *we* were, and so apparently was Hannah. I was positive we'd done something wrong. We could hardly get a cup of milk from her without a struggle.

All goats have a unique voice. It's one way a mother and kid know each other. Our does each had distinct voices we could tell apart without seeing them. Pie had a trumpeting bugle, Nisa a high, skittish whinny. Lizzie's voice was a doleful basso profundo. Hannah's was the loudest and most maudlin, a wheedling falsetto she could turn into a banshee howl. Those afternoons you could hear her up and down the valley. Even our neighbor a half mile away stopped and asked us: What had we done to our goat?

The first few months with the goats had been a joy. But now with the disastrous milkings each morning and evening, the feeding of kids four times a day, the cleaning of bottles and milk pails, and the mucking of the barn—I wasn't quite sure I was cut out for the job. We were milking only one doe back then. How would it work when we were milking four goats, six goats, eight, and feeding twenty kids?

Hannah's constant wailing was the worst. Each afternoon the herd queen stood on the hill and bawled. She was Lucia in the mad scene of *Lammermoor,* Mozart's Queen of the Night. She was Janis Joplin breaking another piece of our hearts each afternoon. I began to wonder along with our neighbor: *What had we done to our goat?*

Withholdings

SHE DIDN'T SETTLE DOWN THE NEXT DAY, NOR THE DAY after. We finally called for help after four days. Mary Beth Bolduc sounded her usual unfazed self on the phone. She agreed to come over on the weekend to see what she could do.

Sunday was hot for May, pink buds on the apple limbs, pale blue sky. Mary Beth arrived before the evening milk when Hannah was bellowing from the hill. Mary Beth tipped her sunglasses down the bridge of her nose.

"Jeez," she said. "I thought you guys were exaggerating."

We brought the milk stand outside for easier inspection. Hannah waddled down the hill at the sight of the stand and waited beside the gate. I let her out and she leaped up and I filled her bucket with grain. Mary Beth sat on the edge of the stand and massaged Hannah's udder for a minute. Confident, slow-moving, Mary Beth Bolduc had a grace around animals that came from years of goat wrangling. Nothing seemed to fluster her. She placed the stainless steel pail on the stand and started to milk, but Hannah kicked. Mary Beth pulled the pail away, talked to Hannah, then started again—

and Hannah kicked. It went like this for a few minutes. Mary Beth tried different positions, but each time she touched Hannah's teats, Hannah lifted her leg. At last Mary Beth elbowed sweat from her forehead.

"I've never seen a doe like this before," she confessed. She draped an arm over Hannah's withers. "What you have here is not a herd queen, but a certified grade-A bitch."

"So we're not crazy?" Dona asked.

Mary Beth jerked her chin at Hannah. "She's the crazy one."

Hannah was licking the last of the grain in her bucket. She backed up to the end of the stand and tugged her head violently against the bars, as if by sheer force she could pull her skull through.

"She's holding back her milk," Mary Beth explained. "She's not letting it down."

We all looked at Hannah. She glanced at us a moment with hazel eyes. Her udder was still engorged, her teats two torpedoes. So she'd been keeping her milk inside her for days, which explained the constant howling. Goats, like all lactating mammals, need a stimulus to let down their milk. The stimulus (usually a suckling baby) triggers hormones—oxytocin, prolactin—in the pituitary gland that then release milk from the udder. The "letdown" lasts about seven minutes in goats, during which time a doe will allow herself to be milked. Since Hannah was a first-time mother in a brand-new herd, she didn't have an older, more experienced doe to mirror, and perhaps didn't know when to let down her milk or *for whom*. Perhaps we weren't providing the correct stimulus. Cows will sometimes save their milk for their calves and not let down their milk for humans. The women herders of Tibet used to blow into the vaginas of their yaks to get their milk to let down.

I started asking Mary Beth questions, but she waved them all away.

"What we need to do now," she said, "is get the milk out of her." Mary Beth leaned into Hannah. "Hannah dear," she whispered. "We're going to have to fix this."

Hannah rolled her eyes and stopped fighting against the headlock and sniffed around for more grain.

Mary Beth asked if we had two lengths of rope or baling twine. She was folding the sleeves of her shirt.

I went to fetch the rope. Mary Beth and Dona consulted. When I returned they'd worked out a plan, and Hannah fought with renewed vigor to get out of the headlock. Dona started making loops with one rope, Mary Beth with the other. I offered to help, but the women were in control. Lola was barking furiously from the house. She must have seen, and sensed, Hannah's distress. Dona cinched loops around Hannah's ankles, threaded the two ropes through diamond-patterned holes on the milk stand. Hannah bucked like a bronco. Dona gripped the ropes in each hand, braced her feet against the legs of the stand, and leaned backward as if water-skiing. Hannah tried to kick but couldn't lift her legs. Mary Beth went to work on Hannah's udder while Dona kept Hannah's legs down with the ropes.

The whole battle lasted about twelve minutes. Hannah wailed through it all. At one point I went inside to settle the dog. When I came out again with a pitcher of water, the women were laved in sweat, and Dona was just letting Hannah back into the barn.

Mary Beth took a glass of water and blew hair from her face. She still couldn't believe our luck; in thirteen years she'd never encountered such a difficult milker. She made us an offer on the spot. She'd take Hannah off our hands for a week and "break" her on her farm and lend us an experienced milker in her stead.

Dona poured a glass of water and thanked Mary Beth. We'd handle the doe, she said. Hannah might be a grade-A bitch—but she was our bitch.

Kids

Lizzie birthed her own twins a week after Hannah's; two doelings, both coffee-colored with white spots. She proved an excellent milker—patient, sturdy on the stand, a slow eater. She allowed us to bottle-raise her babies with no complaint and would lick their butts to stimulate their appetite. What a difference a goat made. She was the complete opposite of Hannah.

Now we were feeding four kids and milking two does. It was mid-May and Hannah's kids were growing fast, Lizzie's catching up. The younger kids mirrored their older pen mates and after a week were already eating grass. We'd begun calling Hannah's copper kid Penny and the black one, the leader of the doelings, Eustace Tilley.

Goats in the wild, like white-tailed deer, hide their kids during the day in "nurseries" while they go off to forage. The doe returns routinely throughout the day to nurse her kids. While left alone under a ledge or fallen tree, the kids sleep, still and silent to not betray themselves to predators. Our own kids behaved in a similar manner the first few weeks. When we milked in the morning and evening they lay inside their pen together in a velvet mass, hidden under a low wooden bench. They didn't move the whole time. But the moment Lizzie, the last milker, went back through the gate and I stood from the stool, all four doelings sprang to life as if an alarm had sounded. Now it was "safe" and they wailed and flung themselves violently against the wire of their pen. They wanted milk.

We'd fashioned a nipple feeder out of a two-gallon plastic bucket: rubber nipples stuck out its sides attached to thin clear plastic tubes that reached to the bottom of the bucket. We'd fill the bucket with fresh milk and the kids would latch on to the nipples and draw milk up through the hoses like sucking through straws. They'd empty the bucket in seconds flat. Dona called the feeder the "suck-it bucket."

Each morning after milking Hannah and Lizzie, the feedings went like this: I poured a quart of milk into the suck-it bucket (the rest we used ourselves). I set the bucket on a low stool about thirty feet from the barn. Then I put away the milk pail and can, the grain bucket, teat dip, and wipes, and swept the milking area. The whole time the doelings piled on each other trying to get out of their pen. When everything was cleaned and put away, I unlatched the kid pen and the doelings flew across the lawn. I had to race them to reach the suck-it bucket first—to hold it down with one hand (lest they knock all the milk over) and with the other hand to help each kid find her own rubber nipple. Usually it meant picking up a frantic kid and placing her in the right spot. Their mouths clamped; tails flicked. They sucked the bucket dry in twenty seconds and I had to pull it away from their fervent mouths. Afterward they stood in sunlight coughing up milk foam, each kid's face painted with a milk mustache—and a beard.

•

Goat kids are born with an undeveloped rumen—the stomach that processes hay and roughage. When they suckle (from a teat or a bottle), they stretch their necks and thereby close the slit in their esophagus, allowing the milk to bypass the first two stomachs and go directly to the third stomach, the omasum. The milk then passes to the fourth stomach, the abomasum. Within a few days after birth, kids nibble bits of grass or hay and their rumens start to grow. At three months, their rumens are fully developed, but kids can be weaned as early as six weeks after birth.

That May we fed our kids three times a day, each about twelve ounces a feed. After a while we judged who needed more (or less) by how they looked. If one of the doelings looked hollow or underfed, we gave her a separate bottle. If one looked fat she got less. Our kids put on about a pound every third day. We'd keep feeding them milk for about ten weeks and wean them at the beginning of July.

Most of the time when they weren't sleeping, the kids played. We fenced off an area outside the barn with plenty of room for them to roam. There they leaped and ran in circles. They sparred and played a kind of tag with the barn door as home base. They climbed onto one another's backs (and ours). Often they'd follow the ringleader, Eustace Tilley, in a conga line and sprint along the top of a stone wall and leap off, one by one, each kid displaying a different dismount—head feint, turn, twist—like miniature gymnasts. We watched their antics for hours.

Word of the kids spread in the valley and soon a steady stream of visitors appeared at our house. The electrician with his daughter showed up unbidden, the FedEx man, the forest ranger and his grandchildren. Everyone came up the hill and asked to see the kids; and since goats got such a bad rap we felt obliged to host a kind of caprine outreach program. It felt those first few weeks as if we were running a petting zoo.

Mid-May we started to drink Hannah and Lizzie's milk. By then their milk had cleared its colostrum stage and the mineral taste—"hormonal," some people call it—that lingers about ten days after giving birth. Filtered and immediately chilled, the milk tasted delicious and hardly different from fresh unpasteurized cow milk. When she didn't kick the pail, Hannah gave an astonishing gallon or more a day. Lizzie gave about three quarts. Of that the kids drank a gallon, which left us with well over a gallon for ourselves each day. Soon it would be time to make cheese.

May flew past and the mountains turned apple green. The kids grew from week to week and called across the lawn. Each morning I milked and fed them and mucked the barn, filled water buckets and mangers, laid down lime and hay. I mended fences and filtered milk and started to make cheese. That spring I sowed three hundred feet of field corn, a hundred feet of beans. Three bushels of potatoes. Onions, tomatoes, cucumbers, squash, fennel, Tuscan kale.

"I did not read books the first summer," Thoreau said about his first year at Walden Pond, "I hoed beans." And so, like him, I didn't have time to read that first spring. I tended goats.

Chèvre

THE EVENING OF MAY 21 I MADE THE FIRST CHÈVRE from our goats' milk. Three gallons of milk sat in a stockpot set inside the kitchen sink. The milk was paper white with a quarter inch of ivory cream floating on its top. Outside, a lazy rain fell across the lawn. I filled the sink with hot water from the tap. The water would act as a warm bath and slowly raise the chilled milk in the pot to the right temperature to make chèvre: between 72 and 86 degrees.

The kitchen windows lay open that evening and the smell of lilacs blew in with the rain. A cardinal sat grooming himself in the lilac bush. I kept checking the milk's temperature every few minutes with a floating thermometer. Finally at 82 degrees I took a foil packet from the freezer—an Abiasa Mesophilic Aromatic Type B culture—and unsealed its top. Inside lay ten grams of freeze-dried bacteria that would convert the sugars in the milk—lactose—into lactic acid. The starter culture looked like powdered yeast and had the pleasant odor of caramel. That evening I was following three slightly different recipes—one from Ricki Carroll's *Home Cheesemaking*, another from a booklet by Benedictine nuns called *Goat Cheese: Small Scale Production.* The third recipe came from Mary Beth Bolduc.

I scooped a quarter teaspoon of the culture from the pack and sprinkled it on the surface of the milk. The powdered bacteria floated like pollen on a lake. Each spore was a little lifeform—*Lactococcus lactis, L. cremoris, L. lactis* subsp. *diacetylactis, Leuconostoc mesenteroides*—that would help acidify the milk and outcompete any unwanted bacteria that might grow in the pot. The spores would also give the curd the characteristic flavor of chèvre. With a long-handled spoon I turned the milk gently over a few times to insinuate the starter throughout. I put the spoon aside and let the milk settle, then covered the pot with its lid.

Milk is mostly water—around 87 percent in cows and goats and humans. Cheesemaking is largely the process of removing water from the solids in the milk. To bind the solids together any number of acidic agents may be used—vinegar, lemon juice, citric acid, thistles. But the most effective coagulant for making cheese (particularly an aged cheese) is rennet, a liquid extracted from the stomach lining of a milk-fed calf, kid, or lamb. How rennet was first discovered is part of cheesemaking apocrypha: a herder in the Near East around 4000 B.C. had to travel a distance in the sun. He poured some morning milk into a pouch made from a calf's stomach. He hiked across the desert. At noon, when he went to drink his milk, he found the liquid had curdled. He had discovered cheese—or at least the rennet used to set it.

Rennet causes the caseins in milk to bind together into a gelatinous mass—a curd. The caseins form "micelles" (small particles of calcium phosphocaseinate) and separate from the whey. The whey, which contains a smaller amount of protein, can be turned into yet another cheese (such as ricotta or the French *brousse*) but the yield is so small, and the labor so great, the whey is often simply composted or fed to pigs—or tossed away.

The rennet I used that evening was a single-strength calf rennet from New England Cheesemaking Supply. It came in a plastic bottle and looked like oolong tea. I filled a juice glass with five tablespoons of cold water, and with a dropper pulled up the smallest amount of rennet from the bottle. I squeezed exactly one drop into the water, stirred the glass, and emptied its contents into the milk. That single drop of rennet would be enough to set the curd for chèvre—rennet is that effective. I spooned the milk again a few times and set the lid on the pot.

The rain picked up now; a chill wind blew through the screens. The milk in the pot needed to stay at a stable temperature—around 72 degrees—through the night. I closed the windows and left the pot alone. The curd would take twelve hours to set up.

The word *chèvre* in French of course means "goat." An appropriate name for a cheese so simple and unmanipulated, it's the closest thing to eating what the goat's been eating—herbs and grasses and hay—transmuted through the art of cheesemaking. Americans knew little about chèvre until fairly recently, partly because cows had always predominated in North American dairies. The cheese industry in America began in the early seventeenth century in the Massachusetts Bay Colony. Puritan cheesemakers brought from their native East Anglia both their breed of cows and their cheesemaking skills. Farmstead cheesemaking in that part of England had recently undergone a tremendous transformation from the small-scale production of diverse fresh cheeses—intended for home use or the local market—to an export industry of hard, durable cheeses that supplied the population of London. The colonial farmers brought to the New World their bias toward hard, exportable cheeses—what became known in time as "English cheese" or "Yankee Cheese," and at last "American cheese." As farmers and cheesemakers spread north and west through the eighteenth and nineteenth centuries, they brought with them the dairying traditions of New England and its penchant for hard English cheese. For good reason: the demand for this type of cheese was enormous. By the start of the nineteenth century New England cheesemakers were shipping close to a million pounds of Yankee cheese each year to the West Indies alone.

Farm women still made delicate fresh cheeses at home. Yet since such cheeses didn't transport well, they were eaten almost exclusively by the farmers, their family, and neighbors. A healthy trade in diverse fresh farmstead cheeses never took hold in the New World, perhaps because the first colonists were English and not French. Chèvre, in particular, didn't catch on because dairying with goats was uncommon (done, if at all, on a small scale by non-English-speaking immigrants). "The goat is the cow of the poor," the old French expression goes; and even though goats were brought over on the *Mayflower,* once they'd done their job of feeding settlers, the ruminant lost favor to the stolid, heavy-producing cow. Soon goats were looked down upon as the animal of subsistence farmers, not as a vehicle for a profitable dairy. "The goat was never well loved by arable farmers on fertile land," writes David Mackenzie. "When agriculture produces crops that man, cow and sheep can consume with more profit, the goat retreats to the mountain tops and the wilderness, rejected and despised—hated, too, as the emblem of anarchy." The goat couldn't compete in the land of the cow and the cowboy. If goats were rejected and despised, "the emblem of anarchy," eating goat cheese became—and even remains in some circles today—synonymous with foreignness, otherness, and snobbery.

I woke early the next morning to check the chèvre. The rain had stopped in the night—the sun was just rising and the leaves of the lilac looked waxed. Dona was already pulling on rubber boots for milking.

In the kitchen the water bath had cooled. I removed the lid from the pot. The odor inside was pleasant and sweet like custard, with a hint of vanilla. The curds lay submerged beneath an inch of clear whey. The whey had a slightly greenish tint, as if the curds were sunk in seawater.

I drained the sink of its cool water, arranged ten tumbler-size molds on the drain board of the sink. The molds were plastic with holes punched in their sides and bottoms. The exciting moment had come; it was time to test the curd.

Most books on cheesemaking describe a technique called the "clean break test" with which the cheesemaker determines if the curds have set up properly. He buries the tips of his fingers an inch beneath the surface of the curd and nudges the index finger ever so slightly upward. A small dome forms and the curd splits on either side of the finger and a "clean break" is made. Photographs of the technique—the finger, the curd, the crack—are confusing because you can't really see the break *happen*. Yet everything about the "clean break" seemed appealing—and somewhat erotic.

I dipped my hand into the curd, palm side up. The curd was seamless and glossy and rather cool. I lifted my index finger;

and as it rose to the surface, the curd split in a straight line, about five inches long. I'd achieved a clean break!

Now I dipped a soup ladle into the curds and filled the molds with the creamy substance. As soon as the curds fell into the tumblers, droplets of whey seeped out the holes in their sides. I ladled more curds into molds, filling one and another to the top; and by the time I got back to the first ones, the curds had sunk, making room for yet more curds. It took ten minutes to completely empty the pot. By now whey leaked from every hole in the tumblers; a clear white rivulet ran into the sink—and pattered down the drain.

In France the curds of farmstead chèvre are typically put in plastic molds or predrained in a cheesecloth, then shaped by hand into small cakes or buttons and turned into "bloomy rind" cheeses such as *crottin* or *cabécou* or *chevrotin*. The cakes, cylinders, cones, or pyramids are salted and set in a well-ventilated drying room, then aged anywhere from a week to a few months. Sometimes the cheeses are sprayed with a mist of white mold (*Penicillium candidum* or *P. camemberti*) or blue mold (*P. roqueforti*), or sometimes the cheesemaker lets the cheeses develop molds on their own from whatever's in the air. The different molds that develop on their rinds impart to the cheeses their own unique flavors. As the cheeses age their crusts become harder and darker—from fr*ais, demi-sec,* and *sec* to *très sec (*fresh, semi-dry, dry, and very dry). Their consistency and color ranges from chalky white to creamy ivory to oozing beige to molten gold.

I didn't intend to age the chèvre I was making. I wanted to eat it fresh. When I finished molding the curds I set a piece of cheesecloth over the tumblers to keep insects away. I opened the window and let in fresh air—the May sun and wind would help the evaporation.

The morning had already begun and Dona was just coming back from milking.

All that morning, the curds drained; the *tap-tap* of dripping whey came from the kitchen sink. My recipes each called for different draining times—six hours or twelve or fourteen; the longer the cheeses drained the drier they'd become. But every aspect of farmstead cheesemaking is so subjective and relies on the particularity of the day, the time, the weather, that recipes are really just signposts and suggestions. Each cheesemaking is different from the last when using fresh raw milk, for the components in the milk change day to day.

By four thirty that afternoon the clouds had gathered again and rain began to fall. I couldn't wait any longer; I was impatient to try the cheese. In the kitchen, I grabbed a plate, turned one of the molds upside down, and tapped its bottom with a finger. The cake slipped out with a little *plop* in a perfect cylinder, moist but firm. I upended another chèvre on the same plate and sprinkled both with kosher salt. The cheeses were still so young the salt immediately drew pebbles of whey to their surface. Outside in the rain I snipped a fistful of chives and minced them on a cutting board back in the kitchen. I rolled one chèvre in a pile of chives, the other in coarse-ground pepper, then set the two cylinders side-by-side on a plate. Dona came into the kitchen and we stood for a long time admiring the chèvres. One green. One black. How many months had they taken to make? Counting the fencing and the barn—over a year. Dona cut thin slices of dark bread my brother, the baker, had sent. Thunder growled outside, the sky turned suddenly tenebrous. I poured two cups of piping tea. The chèvre spread smoothly on the surface of the bread; it *looked* right. The moment at last had come to taste.

A fresh unsalted chèvre curd, only hours after it has been drained, is called in France a *faisselle* after the cups it's drained in. A *faisselle* is not considered yet a cheese; it's more like a mascarpone but lighter, fresher, more subtle. A *faisselle* sits in a cup surrounded by its own whey to keep it moist. You can do anything with it—eat it straight for dessert, mince chives or mint on it, serve it with fruit or berries. A true farmstead *faisselle*—made from raw milk, and only hours old—is difficult to find, even in small village markets in France. In North America, a *faisselle* simply can't be bought or sold, as its milk must be unpasteurized.

The chèvre was so delicious we closed our eyes when we ate it. Because I'd salted the curds it wasn't quite a *faisselle,* yet neither was it properly a cheese, but something between solid and liquid, and as such—sublime.

The rain came harder now. We ate the chèvre, one cake and the other. The chives, the pepper. Then we unmolded a third and poured a pool of honey over the cake and ate it like a dessert, with spoons. Hannah was calling now from the barn; the clock read 4:55. We ate our chèvre and honey and drained more cups of tea; and soon we heard the kids calling too. I fetched the milk pail and can, pulled on rubber boots and a hat, and took one last taste of milk and honey before heading into the rain.

Provender

OUR SIXTY-FIVE-YEAR-OLD NEIGHBOR, JEAN, LIVED ACROSS the notch with a hutch of rabbits, three Morgan horses, some Rhode Island Reds, and an eighty-seven-year-old partner named Jack. She also kept two Saanen goats, pure white does, a Swiss breed with pink noses and little dangling wattles, like earrings, along their necks.

One afternoon late that May, Jean called and said she'd cut her first hay that morning. She planned to get it in the next day. "Two o'clock," she said, "if the weather holds." She didn't need to ask if I'd help.

It takes at the very least two days to put up hay: the first to cut and dry and turn it over with a tedder, the second to ted and dry again, then rake into windrows and bale and transport the bales to the barn. During that time anything can go wrong. The rains come. The wind stops. An afternoon turns muggy. The hay lies damp in the field and rots; or maybe the crop fails in the first place or bindweed invades the field. Or there's a problem with machinery: a piston, a plug, a spring—any number of belts and moving parts that burn or break mid-haying and delay an entire crucial day. Haying requires at least five pieces of large equipment: mower, tedder, rake, baler, flatbed or wagon (not to mention a tractor or two to pull them all). Given the odds of mechanical failure, it's astonishing that people still manage to cultivate and cut and cure and successfully store hay—or that they still bother. But without hay you can't keep hoofed animals. Without hay there's no meat. No milk. No cheese. All flesh begins as grass. Need we be reminded of Whitman's words:

> *A child said,* What is the grass? *fetching it to me with full hands; / How could I answer the child? I do not know what it is any more than he.*

The rains held off all morning, and by three the sun burned hot. Eighty degrees in the shade. Jean had been turning her hay all afternoon with the tedder. She was just hitching the baler to her Farmall. Jack was helping. Tall, strapping, Jack has a head of silver hair and trout brown eyes, but his sight was no longer so good. Most would call him blind.

"Just in time," Jean hailed as she climbed into the high metal seat of her Farmall. "Would you help Jack hitch on?"

She fired the Farmall's engine and the old tractor sputtered to life. Jean wore Bermuda shorts and a white T-shirt. Black Teva sandals. No socks. A ridiculous outfit for haying, one that made me itch all over just to see.

She put the Farmall in gear and backed to the baler. I lined up the tongue of the baler with the drawbar and Jack sank a rusted metal pin. Then Jean climbed from her seat and helped muscle the baler's drive shaft to the PTO on the back of the tractor. I hadn't lifted a single bale yet, but was already drenched in sweat. Jack mopped his forehead with a handkerchief. The air smelled of scorched mint.

The cut hay lay in fluffed windrows around an eight-acre field, narrow runners of emerald green. I walked to the nearest row and grabbed a handful. The grass was dry enough. Sweet smelling. Oregano-ish. A bit bleached of color, but considering all the recent rains, not bad for the first cut of the year.

Jean shouted from the top of the tractor that she was going to bale up a few to see what they looked like. She turned over the PTO and the John Deere baler chugged to life. She rode up along one windrow and the tines of the baler sucked up the hay as if it were a long linen scarf. The plunger mashed the hay into a rectangle; the bale was bound, tied, then inched out the chute and dropped unceremoniously to the ground. Jean braked and shut down the baler and climbed from her seat. I lifted the first bale by its twine to test its weight, the one-hand test. It was easy enough to hold. Light enough. The color pale green, packed tight with hundreds of timothy heads.

Jean lifted the bale herself and made a noncommittal face. "It'll have to do," she said with sudden impatience and climbed back on the tractor. We didn't have all day.

Hay is any number of grasses and herbaceous plants that are cut and dried for fodder. Sometimes a single crop like alfalfa or clover or timothy. Sometimes a mixed crop of whatever happens to be growing in a given field. In New England, hay is generally cut twice a summer, a "first cut" in late spring—usually in June—and a "second cut" in August. First-cut hay tends to be light and stalky; it makes good feed for nonlactating animals that don't require extra energy or protein. Jean's first-cut hay consisted mostly of timothy grass, which was more than adequate for her horses and nonproducing goats.

She made a first pass around the field. The old baler dropped square bales every few minutes. Meanwhile Jack's son Scott had arrived and hitched a flatbed wagon to a red pickup. It was time to start collecting bales. Jack volunteered to drive the pickup.

"You're sure, Dad?" Scott asked.

"Sure I'm sure," Jack blustered and climbed into the cab.

Scott looked at me and shrugged. Jack was a fighter pilot in World War II and flew commercial planes for Pan Am—puddle jumpers—in Central America. He still had the coordinates in his head—longitude and latitude. A Ford pickup with a stick shift was no big deal, especially in a hay field, even if Jack was legally blind.

Scott pulled on cotton gloves and leaped onto the flatbed. I took the field. Jack drove slowly from bale to bale while I swung them up to Scott. The bales weren't bad, forty or fifty pounds; you could take one in each hand. The sun was pale and hot, the color of egg yolk. We had to shout directions to Jack to stop or start, go left or right. It must have been like flying in weather. All he needed was the feel of the wheel and ground control giving him direction.

Jean passed us and nodded approvingly from the throne of her Farmall. Twenty-two years his junior, she'd been with Jack sixteen years—stubbornly unmarried. They'd already chosen their headstones, his standard military, hers with an angel head and shooting star.

Jack stalled the Ford and apologized. Then he almost ran over a bale.

"Dad," Scott yelled. "You're doing remarkably well for a blind man."

"Thank you," Jack shouted.

I'd never met Scott before that day and I yelled into the cab: "Hey, Jack, he looks just like you."

"Who?"

"Your son."

"Well, that's his misfortune," Jack grumbled.

Scott flashed a smile on the flatbed. Jack did too behind the wheel. The two of them back and front, the same crew cut and square jaw. They even had the same teeth.

By the time we'd made the first pass around the field, more neighbors had arrived. Kathy Wagner and Jeannie Zoppel. With five of us the work became easier. Scott spelled Jack in the driver's seat. I climbed on the flatbed to stack. Kathy and Jeannie walked alongside, tossing bales up top. The dePeysters were haying across the notch, and the Lawrences at Polymeadows and the Mattison boys over in Belcher. Everyone taking advantage of the break in weather. Everyone trying to get their hay in before the next rains. They were predicting a storm that evening, which added urgency to the task. The countryside was bringing in the sheaves.

Soon we fell into conversation while the baler chugged in the background and the wagon lurched back and forth and bales came up from left and right. Few of us would get any of Jean's hay; we helped for other reasons. When there's hay to be gotten in, people in the valley join in, whether or not they benefit directly. They do so not for the sake of the person, but for the sake of the hay.

> *I guess it must be the flag of my disposition, out of hopeful green stuff woven. / Or I guess it is the handkerchief of the Lord, / A scented gift and remembrancer designedly dropped . . .*

I like that hay takes precedence when it's ready for cutting, that everything drops away in the valley, even here in the twenty-first century with cell phone towers on the hills and satellites orbiting overhead at night, that the old necessities still bear. I like that for a few weeks in summer, hay is the only news—who's cutting and when and where—that grass is our headlines—*Festuca, Panicum, Avena, Elymus*—what's current and happening—*Poa, Hordeum, Phleum, Agrostis*. Storing summer's wealth is not only important to humans. Beavers drag whole trees underwater in late summer to store in their Frigidaires. Marmots cut and dry mounds of alpine grass for winter. Squirrels, mice, foxes, rats—not to mention all the birds. Who says animals don't have a consciousness about the future? Why else prepare ahead for times to come?

There are good hay years and bad hay years. Years when people miscalculate and mow too early or too late; years when the weather's too wet or too dry. If you don't grow your own hay, finding a good supply can often prove trying. You need to know the hay's provenance, which fields it came from, what kinds of grasses (or fertilizer) went into its making. If the hay lay in the sun too long after mown, it will have been leached of most of its color and nutrients. If it was cut, dried, then rained on and dried *again,* it will be dusty and practically worthless. If it was baled before dry enough it might harbor harmful molds, heat up, and even cause a barn fire. If overhandled the leaves will be frangible or pulverized to dust. All of this you can read into any square bale (and traditional square bales were the only thing we fed our goats; big round bales make a jungle gym for them to climb on). A good bale retains the color of its plants, a deep sage green. You can see the individual dried grasses and legumes packed inside, the leaves and flowers and buds about to bloom; each stalk and bud should look as if it had been lovingly pressed between the pages of a book. You can break open a bale and sniff its vintage and it should smell sweet, like dried marjoram or thyme (or green marijuana). The odor should be so complex and spiced you want to cook with it or eat it or smoke it or rub it in your hair. It should smell, in other words, like food.

Or I guess the grass is itself a child / the produced babe of the vegetation.

The richest hay—second-cut hay—is mown late in summer when the grass and legumes are about to bloom and reach the peak of their protein content. At that stage, grasses contain the most carotene, sugars, ascorbic acid, and vitamin B—all of which decrease as the plants mature and turn fibrous and stalky. Second-cut hay tends to have more leaves and flowers than first-cut. Because the days are shorter in August, and the sun less hot that time of year, it takes more time to cure second-cut hay—usually four days to be safe. Our goats prefer a second-cut hay, especially when they're lactating. If we give them a bale of first-cut timothy, unless they're absolutely starving, they'll sniff the dry stems and walk away. If we offer a green, leafy second-cut clover or alfalfa, they'll devour it in great mouthfuls and fight over every leaf. All hay is not equal, and the difference is not only in taste. Alfalfa, for example, has almost three times as much protein as timothy; and a properly harvested hay can have more than twice as much protein as a poorly harvested one. Poor hay produces poor milk, poor cheese—and potentially sick animals. When we feed our does quality hay they eat less and maintain their weight. On poor hay, they eat and eat, looking for minerals and proteins—and still grow thin.

I once stood before a wall of hay at the West Virginia State Fair. Twenty square bales were competing for blue ribbons.

They stood stacked upon each other in the center of an enormous fair building. Each bale had its own distinct texture and color, and the shades ran from ecru to rosemary to bright cucumber green. Each bale looked like an enormous paint swatch, yet if you walked up close, you could see on the surface individual pressed flowers as if freeze dried just before their bloom: here a blood-red dot of clover. There the Dutch pink of alsike. Here the cadmium yellow of birdsfoot trefoil or the deep purple of vetch. Each bale looked painted by a pointillist.

We made our first trip to Jean's barn, unloaded the bales, and drove back for another load. The sun lolled in the west. It was five o'clock and still torrid. More neighbors had arrived and were stacking another wagon they'd brought along. Jean was almost done now baling the last of the windrows, but plenty bales still sat as monoliths in the field. By now my T-shirt hung sopped to clavicles. I was sticky and itchy all over. I try to cover every inch of skin when I'm haying—long-sleeve shirt, gloves, socks, boots, bandana for neck and over mouth—but it never seems to help. The hay gets everywhere, especially in the lungs.

Kathy Wagner was up high on the flatbed now, Scott and I tossing her bales from below. We were up to 290 (the counter on the baler told us so). The wind picked up as if a large fan had been switched on across the field. At the far, shady end of the meadow the bales grew heavier and moister. The moister bales might prove problematic drying in the barn, but Jean figured she'd take the risk. Her horses weren't nearly as fussy as our goats. Tossing the heavy bales proved harder—especially because we were tired by then. I warned Kathy, who had to lean over to catch them. She gave me a look as if to say, we'll see about that. Kathy stands over six feet tall. Lean, muscular, she's a former U.S. Army kickboxing champion.

She handled the bales with aplomb.

Before World War II, hay making determined the rhythm of North Americans' summers. The long summer school holiday was first instituted in the States largely because of the need for children to help put up summer's hay. Without all the tractors and balers and tedders, the labor of hay making took several days or weeks. If hay making today seems quaint, an antique relic, it's only because we keep so many of our hoofed animals hidden behind factory walls and feed them things they were never meant to eat—like corn. That hay translates directly into milk and meat and bone seems today an abstraction. Ask most urbanites about a hay field, and they'll have no idea what it's actually for.

> *Or I guess it is a uniform hieroglyphic / . . . Sprouting alike in broad zones and narrow zones . . .*

The first time I ever went haying was in West Virginia. My brother lived on a family farm in Summers County. The couple that owned the place had come from far corners of the earth, he from a city in East Germany near the Baltic Sea, she from Tehran. They raised their own vegetables, cattle, chickens, and horses. They also kept Nubian goats. What they were doing in those isolated hills wasn't clear to me at first; their kind of life was new to me at the time.

For a week we waited to get in the hay. When it was mown and finally dry enough, when the afternoon at last came, more help arrived and suddenly we were a team—the couple and their two young daughters, my brother and myself, and the retired mountaineers, Bud and Ethel, who lived on the neighboring land. All of us drove up a path to a field near Bud and Ethel's house to get the hay in before nightfall.

I remember the light that afternoon on the newly cut field. That sharp after-a-storm sky and clean unfiltered light that carves into hills and picks out every rock and stone. On the hay field the light seemed to float like a presence animating everything—the red tractor, the green hay bales, each of us gathered there in an odd convocation of old and young. Germans. Iranians. Appalachians. My brother and myself, Jews from suburban New York City. We worked for hours in that slender orange glow as if suspended in amber solution, walking in and out of emerald swathes and lime green stubble. We worked until evening and salt burned our faces, but I recall a joy I'd never experienced before, as if I'd found some calling or communion I hadn't known existed. My muscles ached and hay chafed each part of my body. By the third load darkness fell and we breathed clouds of moisture into the damp and two ponies trotted down from the woods and watched us. They whinnied at the sight of so much hay and followed us along a fence line, tails flicking high. We got the last bales in as a brass moon popped above the field, and we raced the truck through dusk up to a pond in a higher pasture. And there all eight of us stripped and plunged into the water, yelling because it was so cold, and coming out—shivering—a chorus of chattering teeth.

Later, back at the couple's house, the German's grandmother ladled a venison roast marinated in buttermilk and wine, and there were enormous platefuls of potatoes and carrots and apfelkuchen. We drank a lot of wine, and grew lightheaded from the icy water, bone-tired from the haying. The grandmother kept pushing more apfelkuchen on us—

die letzte Stück, ein mehr—until we were all laughing in gasps at her persistence.

The day left a deep impression. The light on the field, the children carrying bales across the swathe, the Iranian woman up top tucking in the last green bale. The barn loft filling bale by bale. The roast afterward. I slept better that night than in years. Not because the hay was mine or I knew the animals or that I had a stake in any of it. But because I'd been a part of that time and place, in concert with the season and earth, a participant in one of the oldest pastoralist events. When I boarded the train back to Penn Station two days later, something had changed. I understood at last why the German and Iranian decided to live in the middle of nowhere, and not in their respective cities. I've had times haying since that seemed like grace, the last load coming in just before a storm. But I remember that first haying the most as revelation.

> *Growing among black folks as among white, / Kanuck, Tuckahoe, Congressman, Cuff . . . / And now it seems to me the beautiful uncut hair of graves.*

We loaded the last wagon into Jean's barn. I stayed outside on the flatbed, tossing bales down to Kathy, who threw them up to Scott, who stacked them deep in the recesses of the barn. It was near six now. Still hot. Bits of chaff floated in stabs of light. The hay caught in the back of my throat. The inside of the barn was a dark theater, a suspension of time and place, a silver gelatin print. This scene which could've been caught one or two hundred years before—save Jean's Tevas and sunglasses and nylon cap and, of course, the truck.

•

The dreams of pastoralists have always involved grass: meadows, mountain pastures. Rolling prairies. Our love of green lawns and open fields may well reach back to the savannah where we first emerged as walking hominids, able to see both predator and prey at long distances. Pastoralists took this love of grass to another level, because of their utter dependence upon it. The first nomadic pastoralists dreamed of a perennially green land, a place they could lead their flocks to with good forage. An Arcadia, a land of milk and honey. A paradise.

The nomadic dream is to follow an ever-unfolding bloom. To walk or ride alongside hoofed animals and lead them to provender. The enduring myth of the cowboy is just the latest incarnation of the nomad leading his animals to pasture, providing food, and protecting his herds against the wild. The Indo-European root word *pa* ("to feed, protect") holds within its kernel the germ of that dream, and all the words that sprout from it—*food, fodder, feed, foster, pasture, repast, pasta, pabulum, pantry, pasture, company, companion*—tell the same story: of provision and protection. Companionship with other animals and other humans.

After the last load we headed back to Jean's house. It was early evening. Shadows encroached on the field. A bank of rose-colored thunderheads towered in the south; but the rains had kept off, and for that everyone was glad. We gathered momentarily inside Jean's hot kitchen—sweaty, chaff sticking to arms and necks. If it had been another time or place, there might've been a celebration, a ritual, a roast, or a song—a meal at the very least. But this was frugal New England. Instead of the raucous meal, the beer or wine, Jean thanked us and smilingly handed each of us a small green bottle of

Vermont Sweetwater, a drink made of maple sap. It was carbonated, nonalcoholic. Cold and parsimonious—but also: delicious.

I drank the bottle in one go.

Before I climbed back into my truck I took one bale I'd stowed earlier that afternoon. A two-by-four-foot token of the day. I'd wait until a February snowstorm to break it open for the goats. The sound goats make when eating green hay is a kind of champing music: *croop, croop, croop.* Lovely to hear. If they really like the hay they make happy nickering sounds while eating. I didn't think they'd make those sounds with this timothy hay, but I wanted a reminder nonetheless. A memory of that day preserved in grass. I'd take it out in the cold of winter and think, here it is, that day of sunlight and grass in June. A reminder that *a leaf of grass is no less than the journey-work of the stars.*

The Milk Diary

BY THE END OF MAY, HANNAH AND LIZZIE SETTLED into a routine. Lizzie was wonderful to milk, but Hannah never easy. If I didn't empty her quick enough she kicked. If she didn't like the amount of grain in her bucket she kicked. If she was almost finished with her grain she learned she could get more—if she kicked. I had to be swift and awake and anticipate her every move. It didn't help that I usually milked at first light just after I'd crawled from bed.

I took the morning milkings, Dona the evening. The days were long then, the valley aqua blues and green. It rained often and thunderstorms raced up the valley and twice a rainbow appeared above the house. I made chèvre and a simple mozzarella that Mary Beth taught me to make. I started keeping a journal that spring, a diary, a log with amounts of milk and cheeses made. The journal grew longer and became, in time, an inquiry into the idea of paradise. I called it the Milk Diary.

Only two letters unyoke the words *diary* and *dairy* yet their roots remain stubbornly unrelated. Milk and ink. One went in a bucket. The other in a journal. I sat down to both each day.

MAY 31

Six a.m. Pink clouds, wet grass. I cross the lawn; the milk pail creaks. The goats call from the barn: Milking time!

I set up the grain bucket, the scoop, the stool. The kids lie curled inside their pen. Hannah, the queen, milks first. She jumps up to the stand, dives into her grain, and her head locks into place. I clean her teats with an antiseptic wipe and start to milk.

Hannah is in good spirits this morning. I milk her out with no struggle, pour her four quarts into a stainless steel milk can. I bend beneath her belly with a bottle of blue antibacterial teat dip, raise its cupped lid over one teat then the other. She winces at the cold dip. I release the headlock and she pulls out and stands a moment while I scratch her cheeks. She licks her lips, then licks my chin, before she goes back through the gate.

Lizzie's been waiting patiently the whole time. She leaps up next. Her body smells of hair and hide and something slightly oily but not unpleasant. I lean my forehead into her orange flanks and she leans back; and after a few seconds, I feel her milk let down. Small explosions rumble in her stomach, her rumen contracting every sixty-three seconds. Beside my ear, her body sounds like the ocean.

MORNING	EVENING
1½ gallons	1 gallon

- Mucked barn.

JUNE 1

Goats have two teats (cows have four). To milk a goat you grasp a teat in each hand and work the liquid from the udder. You start with the thumb and press on the teat with each successive finger until you've reached your pinkie. Imagine playing each ivory on a piano. Thumb to pinkie. Thumb to pinkie. Only the keyboard is in the shape of a cone. You press those five notes over and over using both hands: one going up the scale, the other going down.

The music is milk in a pail.

Problems occur if the doe's teats are small and your hands too large, or if you don't open your thumb and index finger wide enough at the start of the stripping; or if you impede the flow of milk at the bottom of the teat by closing it off with your pinkie. The hardest thing to learn is how to relax and let your hands be a conduit for the milk. It's easy to stop the flow. Breathing helps, singing does too.

The muscles used for milking—the forearm flexors—are the same employed by bakers who knead by hand. The word *dairy* comes from the Indo-European root *dheigh,* which means "to knead." The treading action kittens make to stimulate their mother's milk. The action my hands make on Hannah's teats. The word *dough* also comes from *dheigh.*

So does the word *paradise.*

MORNING	EVENING
1½ gallons	1 gallon

- Cleaned kid pen.
  Spread lime.

JUNE 2

Rain again. An oyster sky. The barn fills with a slick of mud and the goats can't go to pasture. The queen complains the most. Up on the stand this morning she finished her grain in record time and I wasn't quick enough to move the pail and—*splat*—she stuck her hind foot into her gallon of milk. The queen looked back at me and batted her golden lashes. I had to toss the milk.

Some mornings (when she doesn't kick the pail) Hannah's been giving over a gallon of milk, remarkable for a first-time freshener and a Nubian goat, a breed not known as big producers. Saanen and Alpine goats tend to give more milk, but theirs has less butterfat than Nubian milk. Still, Hannah and Lizzie are large goats (about 150 pounds now—they'll continue to grow for another two years) and they have the advantage of a virgin pasture and endless spring-green leaves.

A gallon of goat milk weighs 8.6 pounds, which means we've been getting 21.5 pounds of milk on a good day; half of that goes to feed the kids.

Paradise was originally pictured as a park, garden, or hunting reserve populated by abundant friendly animals. It often featured rivers of honey, milk, or wine. The word literally means "enclosed garden" from the Hebrew and Persian *pardes* and the Greek *paradeisos*. *Paradise* came to mean any place of ideal beauty, but also a state of delight.

MORNING	EVENING
¾ gallon	¾ gallon

- Made chèvre from four gallons.

JUNE 4

That fine gazelle, that fawn sent
To torture lovers with endless grief,
Heard me complain my soul was faint
With desire for her, and offered: "My saint,
If inside me you feel it's too tight for you—
Loosen up and you'll find your relief."

—TODROS ABULAFIA,
THIRTEENTH-CENTURY SPAIN

In medieval Hebrew poetry, the gazelle, the doe, the deer, and the fawn were used as stand-ins for "the lover" or "the beloved." The gazelle motif sprang from earlier Arab poetry and also from the Old Testament's Song of Solomon ("My beloved is like a gazelle"). Both Arab and Hebrew gazelle poems were often unabashedly erotic; they told of longing and illicit love doomed to failure. The gazelle was sometimes a metaphor for God.

Gazelles and goats come from the same taxonomic order, the artiodactyls—even-toed ungulates—and the same suborder: Ruminantia, or ruminants. Goats are barnyard antelopes. They're working-class gazelles.

MORNING	EVENING
1¼ gallons	¾ gallon

- Mucked barn; limed; washed milking area.

JUNE 7

Each morning I carry milk across the lawn. The milk keeps warm in a three-gallon stainless steel milk can. I haul the can by its handle into the kitchen, then strain the milk through a four-inch-wide cotton filter. The filter picks up any stray hairs or blood clots from Hannah's or Lizzie's teat cisterns. I filter the milk into clean bottles and chill it immediately in the freezer, or put it directly in a pot if I'm making cheese. The FDA's *Grade "A" Pasteurized Milk Ordinance,* Item 18r under Section 7, stipulates that dairies must chill their milk to forty-five degrees within two hours after milking. Big dairies have bulk tanks that cool the milk and keep it until a milk truck arrives that day or the next day, or the day after. From there the milk travels to a central plant that may be as far as several states away.

Our milk doesn't have to travel far from its source—just one hundred feet into the house. It's one advantage, of many, we have over an industrial dairy. Our milk is local and autochthonous. It never leaves the place where it was born.

Rain again today, the meadow is a sponge. The barn reeks of urine and soaked hay. I long for the sun to appear. The goats, I imagine, do too.

MORNING	EVENING
1¼ gallons	¾ gallon

- Made mozzarella from five gallons.

JUNE 8

A cold wind punched from the west this afternoon and the clouds fled overhead. At last, the day turned brilliant. I belled the does and let the kids in with them. Lizzie sniffed her spotted twins and licked their butts. Hannah paid no attention to her kids. Pie, the yearling, rammed Penny—Hannah's copper doeling—who screamed and ran between my legs for protection. Everyone was eager to get out into the sparkling lawn.

I opened the gate and the goats loped toward Mason's Hill. The kids called and sprang in the tall grass. The adults ate everything in sight. Spirea and wild strawberry; cinquefoil and raspberry vines. They shouldered each other aside like bargain hunters at a sample sale. Hannah sought dandelion heads. Nisa swung her head like a mine sweep in the grass. Pie lifted on hind legs for a birch leaf. Penny stayed between my legs. She's the runt, and the most affectionate of the kids. When I sat on the hill, she stepped into my lap and lay there for fifteen minutes while the others roved and gorged. Clouds sailed overhead like spinnakers. I watched them heading eastward toward the sea.

MORNING	EVENING
1¼ gallons	1 gallon

- Planted summer lettuces.

JUNE 9

The sky sea green at six a.m. Drizzle on new leaves. My queen cries from the barn: *Milk me!* When she sees me in the bedroom window, her pleas double to commands.

I, good servant, obey.

This morning, udder engorged, she made a field goal attempt at the pail, yet I caught her leg in time. *Aha! Outdone, my liege*. No extra point for you!

The Bible tells exactly where Paradise lay. The river that flowed from Eden became the Tigris and Euphrates, which places the original paradise in Mesopotamia—right in modern-day Iraq.

Eve and Adam gathered wild food in Paradise. They needed neither to sow nor hunt nor herd animals. Yet once expelled from Eden they had to till the ground "in the sweat of thy brow." The first couple were forced into the transition made by humans in the Near East during the so-called Neolithic revolution: they became farmers.

It's telling how the change from subsistence gathering to farming (the "revolution") was viewed in Genesis as a decline in living standards: as a punishment. In spite of how we've dismissed hunter-gatherer cultures in the last several centuries as "primitive" and "savage," the Bible is quite clear on the subject: Paradise was a place populated by gatherers.

MORNING	EVENING
2 gallons!	1 gallon

- Made chèvre from 4½ gallons.

JUNE 12

The valley this morning is a Japanese print: Blue cloud. White mist. Spruces half hidden in fog. We've been milking now for over six weeks. It gets easier with time; even the queen seems content.

This morning I thinned the kids' milk with a few cups of water. It makes the milk less appealing—and quickens the weaning process. In two days I'll add more water to the suck-it bucket, and then even more, until the kids eventually lose their taste for watered-down milk. We've been supplementing their diet with a scoop of pelleted grain, and they're almost as excited by the rattle of grain in a bucket as the shake of the suck-it bucket's handle. In two more weeks, they'll be completely off milk, just in time for Independence Day.

MORNING	EVENING
1¾ gallons	1 gallon

- Penny has an abscess on her upper lip. Applied a hot compress.

JUNE 14

We placed advertisements yesterday for the kids. "Kids for Sale. American Nubian Doelings," read the ads. "Bottle-raised babies. Black and white. Brown. Polka dot." We ran them in several local papers.

We'd love to keep all four kids but don't have room in the barn. We're thinking about keeping Hannah's twins—Penny and Eustace Tilley—because they're our first. But we need to find a home for Lizzie's spotted doelings where they'll be kept together. Kids form fierce attachments to one another and to place. If you remove a kid from her herd and put her with unfamiliar goats where she doesn't have a pal, she'll become hazardously stressed. She'll scream so loud and long, she'll lose her voice.

The Bible begins with loss—expulsion from Paradise—and exile runs throughout the five books of Moses: Eden. Canaan. Zion. A serial ordeal of exiles, a perennial diaspora from paradise. But was it an actual *place* lost, a piece of real estate, or a state of mind?

MORNING	EVENING
1½ gallons	¾ gallon

- Abscess still on Penny's lip. Treated with ichthamol cream. Cleaned and limed kid pen. Made mozzarella from five gallons.

JUNE 15

Dairying is a kind of violence. Even here in the best of circumstances. To get milk from our goats we create a state of enforced nursing. We impregnate our does, steal their babies, and sell them to strangers. However peaceful my morning milkings, however content the does, there is coercion. Dona says we run a women's prison. Hannah may be the queen but we're the jailers.

MORNING	EVENING
¾ gallon	1 gallon

- Hannah kicked pail.

JUNE 16

Gandhi was so distressed by the maltreatment of dairy cows in India that he vowed never to drink milk or eat its byproducts. For years he searched for an alternative to animal milk and wrote about his experiments with a milk-free diet. Yet his health was never good, and at forty-eight he fell dangerously ill. His wife, Kasturba, and his doctors urged him to break his vow and take milk; he needed the animal protein, they said, but Gandhi refused. "I feel it better to die than to break a vow knowingly and deliberately taken," he wrote.

In a fit of frustration Kasturba asked Gandhi: If his vow was against drinking cow and buffalo milk, why wouldn't he drink the milk of a *goat*? Gandhi, a lawyer, puzzled over this for days. Finally he found no defense and reluctantly agreed. He drank goat milk. It saved his life.

"The goat has proved a mother to me," he wrote later, and when the worst of his illness passed he penned a lighthearted poem to his son about his doe:

Rasiklal Harilal Mohandas Karamchand Gandhi
Had a goat in his keeping;
The goat would not be milked
And Gandhi would not stop his weeping.

Once he drank goat's milk, Gandhi traveled everywhere with his doe—even on a state visit to London. He and the she-goat traveled together on a ship. She provided him with his only animal food. It's said he often called off meetings with dignitaries to milk her. Hers were the only mammaries that Gandhi, celibate from age thirty-six, touched for decades.

MORNING	EVENING
1¾ gallons!	1 gallon

- Kids knocked over suck-it bucket.
  Fed grain. Abscess still on Penny.

JUNE 18

Trimmed hoofs this morning. When hoofs become overgrown they're hard to walk on and eventually will cripple a goat. Here in wet and wooded New England, goats' hoofs don't get worn down the way they would on rock cliffs, ledges, and scree. Nothing wears them down but us—every few weeks or so.

I trimmed Nisa's and Pie's. Dona did Lizzie's and Hannah's. Our hoof trimmer looks like stubby pruning shears. We put Nisa in the stand, gave her grain to busy herself. I stood facing backward and bent her foreleg behind her and up to face the sky. With the pointed end of the trimmer, I scraped away mud and manure to reveal the surface of the foot. A goat's foot is designed like a suction cup, with a hard outer hoof wall for gripping steep ledges, and a soft rubbery interior for absorbing the shock of leaps. The outer wall is black, the interior and heel—the "frog"—white. I pared down the overgrown outer wall so it lay in a straight plane, then snipped the tips of the toes, cutting back to reveal fresh white growth. Then came the hard part—the frog—slicing it down so it lay flat and even with the outer hoof. I needed to use an eight-inch plane to flatten and smooth each hoof. I rasped the plane back and forth, while white shavings piled up on the floor as if from a Parmesan. I tried to make the bottom of each hoof flat as an iron.

Pie and Nisa and Lizzie all have good hoofs, but Hannah's hoofs are terrible. Her toenails curve up in the front like elfin shoes and she has excess frog growth in the back, so she walks as if on pumps. We've been trying to correct her feet for months. Today we both had to work on her, because she hates having her hoofs trimmed. She stamps and bucks. Everything about the queen is excessive, including her feet.

Afterward, Dona trimmed the kids' hoofs. She sat in the grass and flipped one on her back into her lap and scissor-gripped the kid between her legs. Each kid protested at first before they submitted. Four legs stuck up in the air like a candelabra. The bottoms of their hoofs are the size and shape of guitar picks.

The poet Donald Hall, incidentally, calls the strong rhythm of a poem its "goat foot."

MORNING	EVENING
1½ gallons	1 gallon

- Made chèvre from five gallons.

JUNE 20

Tardy to milk this morning: the queen was cross. Halfway through milking she dipped her hoof into the pail. I had to toss her milk.

No use crying over spilled milk and *kicking the bucket* must have been chestnuts uttered often by dairy farmers before the advent of milking machines. Kicking the bucket does mean a kind of sudden death—no milk to be had that day.

If farming was viewed in Genesis as a step down—a punishment—from the hunter-gatherer's lifestyle, there may have been good reason. Farming required hard work. People had to cut open the earth and coax enough vegetable protein from it to feed themselves. Yet there was a third option open to humans, neither hunting-gathering nor farming: pastoralism. Jim Corbett, the Quaker cofounder of the Sanctuary Movement and author of the book *Goatwalking,* says that nomadic pastoralism developed in reaction to the failure and destructiveness of settled agriculture—which always led to centralized warring nation-states. People with goats and sheep and horses simply turned their backs on it all, took their herds, and went walking. "A symbiotic relationship with ruminants," he writes, "opens an unguarded back gate to Eden . . . For the farmer, food is necessarily the product of labor. For the herder, food is a gift, eternally regenerating itself."

MORNING	EVENING
¾ gallon	1 gallon

- Cleaned and limed barn.
  Penny's abscess drained!

JUNE 25

I mucked the barn this morning. At 8 a.m. I locked the does outside and pitchforked heavy damp mats of hay and feces into a waiting wheelbarrow, walked it across the lawn, and dumped the matting in the garden to decompose. I had to make eight trips across the lawn, then scraped and swept and sifted lime over the floorboards. An hour later, my T-shirt was drenched and boots coated with muck. I poured water over my head from a garden hose.

Manure presents the most work, the heavy lifting. It limits the number of goats we'll ever keep. More does, more manure. Every six weeks in winter we spend a whole morning shoveling and forking decomposing hay from the barn. It's backbreaking work; and then we have to find a place to put it all. Manure may be unavoidable, but it's also a kind of wealth. In rural Sweden people once judged a family's fortune by how big their dung pile was each spring. The larger the pile, the more fertile their crops that year. Milk and manure—you can't have one without the other.

Goat feces makes great compost. I've been putting their waste directly in the garden since last fall, and already have noticed the garlic and onions and beets are plumper than ever before. Unlike cow and horse manure, goat feces is relatively free of weed seeds, but the hay it's mixed with *is* full of seeds.

Goat dung is odorless and relatively dry. The pellets are round—the size of jelly beans—and roll off whatever they hit. They break down in a few days to dust. Goat urine smells like hops, not unpleasant at first, but after a few days in the barn, the bottom layer of hay turns into a manure tea. When I pitchfork a heavy mat of urine-soaked hay, the smell is like ammonia and stale beer.

The poet Allen Ginsberg, who briefly milked goats in upstate New York in the 1960s, wrote to his friend Gary Snyder at the time: "I keep straying on mental anger warpaths, then come back to milking goats."

MORNING	EVENING
1½ gallons	¾ gallon

- Mucked barn.

JULY 3

Our milk stand is welded iron, painted rustproof black. The stand is slightly smaller than a yoga mat and larger than a *sajjada,* a Muslim prayer mat, but serves a similar function. A prayer mat is a physical reminder to place yourself in the world; and, while on it, direct your thoughts to God. A prayer mat (like a flying carpet) transports its user to a "higher" plane. The true believer stands with his hands crossed at the wrists and eyes closed. The Yogi sits in a lotus position. The meditating Buddhist sits on a *zafu.* Each has their square or circle of fabric to remind them where to be. I sit on a milk stand with a goat.

The mystical collection of the Jewish Kabbalists, the Zohar, interprets the Torah in four different ways: The simple and literal meaning (Peshat). The meaning through hints and allusions (Remez). The meanings through interpretation (Derash). And the secret and mystical meaning (Sod). After decades of study when a kabbalist finally understands all four interpretations, he reaches enlightenment. The initial letters of each of the words for understanding—*P*eshat, *R*emez, *D*erash, and *S*od—spell *P'RDES.* In Hebrew *pardes* means "paradise." For the mystical Jew—already exiled and landless—Paradise was found not in a place, but inside a book.

MORNING	EVENING
1¼ gallons	⅞ gallon

- One of Lizzie's twins has scours (diarrhea). Normal temperature. Offered baking soda. Scrubbed kid pen.

JULY 5

This morning I gave the kids no milk. They ran out of their pen, searched high and low for the suck-it bucket; not finding it, they rushed to their grain trough and fought for the few oats I'd put there. Each kid weighs about twenty-five pounds now and they've been eating grass and hay for weeks. Still, they miss their milk; they've been crying all afternoon.

Is earthly paradise found, as Eduardo Galeano writes, "on the nipple of a woman's breast"? Is that the place we're always trying to get back to, our original paradise?

MORNING	EVENING
1½ gallon	¾ gallon

- Scours still. Fed Pepto-Bismol. Temperature normal. Fed dry hay.
  Made chèvre from five gallons.

JULY 7

I couldn't get the milk out of Hannah's left teat this morning. The right teat was fine, but the left blocked. No matter how hard I squeezed, the milk wouldn't flow normally, but sprayed in a thin fan all over the side of the pail and on my jeans. My arms grew weak. I broke into a sweat. The queen launched milk all over the floor. Field goal. I had to fill her grain twice before I milked her out.

Mary Beth says she may have mastitis, or perhaps a "milk plug" or "milkstone," a fleshy buildup blocking the orifice. This evening, both Dona and I went out to investigate. Hannah took the stand. Dona went to milk and had the same problem.

I brought out the California Mastitis Test Kit and handed Dona its white plastic paddle. She squeezed milk from Hannah's left and right teat into corresponding cups on the paddle. I squirted one pumpful of the kit's reagent—a pH indicator—into the left and right cups, swirled the paddle so the liquids combined. If the milk formed a gel with the purple reagent, it would indicate the presence of a high number of somatic cells, namely mastitis—yet no gel formed. We repeated the process twice to make sure. Negative both times. I wasn't surprised. Hannah seemed healthy otherwise. What could be stopping her milk?

MORNING	EVENING
¾ gallon	¾ gallon

- Scours cleared. Mucked barn.

JULY 8

The problem with Hannah persists—this morning a disastrous milking, her teat still blocked. Afterward, I pored over the section on "Teat Obstruction and Stenosis" in Smith and Sherman's *Goat Medicine*. Milkstones are small hard concretions floating in the teat cistern, read the manual. They may work as a ball valve and shut off the opening of the teat. "Stones that cannot be forcibly expressed from the teat or crushed with alligator forceps could be removed surgically."

We've been trying to find a good goat vet for months. I've called around a half dozen places. There are plenty of vets in the area for horses, cattle, dogs, and cats, but vets who specialize in goats are rare. The practice in Granville that Mary Beth uses is too far from our farmstead. We could take Hannah there in the car, and it might come to that. We'll see what happens tomorrow morning.

"Men are not so much the keepers of herds," writes Thoreau, "as herds are the keepers of men."

MORNING	EVENING
¾ gallon	½ gallon

JULY 9

We both went out to milk this morning—nervous master and mistress—expecting the worst. Hannah took the stand, Dona the stool. After the first faint squirts of milk, Dona gently rolled Hannah's left teat between her palms as if making sausage; after a minute a small fleshy piece of tissue extruded from the orifice. Pink, squamous, the size of a split pea—the milkstone!

Then Hannah's milk flowed unstoppered, abundant. *Hallelujah*!

Even Hannah seemed grateful. She didn't stomp or kick and afterward went back through the gate and took a long drink from the bucket, lifted her head, and watched us, water glistening from her golden beard.

The gate that was shut—oh
Arise and open it! The gazelle that ran
Away—oh send him to me! On the day
You come to me and lie between my
Breasts. Your fragrance will rest upon
Me.

—SOLOMON IBN GABIROL,
ELEVENTH-CENTURY GRANADA

MORNING	EVENING
2½ gallons!	1 gallon

- Scrubbed and limed kid pen.
  Made chèvre from four gallons.

JULY 16

In Arabic a gazelle can mean both an animal and a poem. The poetic *ghazal* has a unique and complex form believed to have originated among Bedouin herders around the seventh century. The poem, which is made up of a series of couplets called *shers* and a rhyming refrain at the end of each couplet called a *radif,* can be a form of clever sparring—a poetic challenge; but more often a *ghazal* is an erotic poem: one about longing for an impossible person or place.

Once a poet sets up the *radif* it must be repeated at the end of each couplet. Tension builds by the audience waiting to see how the poet will resolve—and make new—the same ending. "The alluring tension," said the poet Agha Shahid Ali, "of a slave trying to master the master."

How is my queen like a poem? A *slave trying to master the master*. But who is master and who is slave? Who builds up tension and then—release?

A *ghazal* has at least five couplets, but there's no limit. A *ghazal* can go on forever.

MORNING	EVENING
1¾ gallons	1 gallon

- Made mozzarella from five gallons.

JULY 17

I milked goats this morning, and this afternoon I tried my hand at a gazelle.

A *Ghazal for* Hannah

My Queen my hart why shouldn't we love
On a hill on a sward with all your four feet

Come my hind who cares what they say
The moon lays its swords across your four feet

Artiodactyl antilopinae
Turn your lyre and tune your four feet

My measure you don't like my dactyls my limbs?
Would you love me better if I had more feet?

What matters my form if we're the same matter
My ayelet *my camel* are you getting cold feet?

Enough now! We're a couplet (though you say we're just friends)
If we join together we'll stand on more feet

Come lay your muzzle beside me and nuzzle
My gazelle—my goat—implore your four feet

Dawn lights the east the time's almost lost
Fall on the floor and raise your four feet!

What? You turn cheek and sashay away
And stand me up here on my two poor feet

MORNING	EVENING
¾ gallon	1 gallon

- Hannah stepped in pail.

JULY 18

A beloved gazelle, a graceful mountain-goat;
let her breasts satisfy you at all times,
be infatuated with love of her always

—PROVERBS 5:19

Galactopoietic may be the most beautiful word in English. It comes from the Greek *gala,* for "milk" or "milky" (as in *galaxy* or *milky way*), plus *poiesis*—to "make or create" (as in the word *poet*).

My doe is galactopoietic; she has the ability to produce milk. Does that make her, like all nursing mothers, a poet of milk?

The Zohar calls the gazelle "the Glory of God."

MORNING	EVENING
2 gallons	1 gallon

JULY 20

The days grow bleached and glaucous. Almost 95 today at noon. The goats swelter; flies buzzsaw. I've been cleaning the barn every other day but it doesn't seem to help. I hang a fan in the doorway high enough so the weanlings won't chew the cord. The queen stands in its slipstream, air folding back long white ears, her retainers at her sides. We've been putting vegetable oil on her grain and her coat has turned molten, lit from within. A golden raiment. The queen loves a palanquin, but the electric fan will do.

One recurring element of paradise myths found in parts of Africa, wrote the scholar Mircea Eliade, is the close proximity of paradise to earth, how back in mythic time, people could easily get from one to the other by climbing a tropical tree or vine or scaling a mountain or ladder. Some cataclysmic event—a flood or an earthquake—severed the tie between heaven and earth. Yet paradise can be attained anew through shamanistic ritual. "In numerous traditions," noted Eliade, "friendship with animals, knowledge of their language . . . are so many signs that the shaman has reestablished the 'paradisal' situation lost at the dawn of time."

MORNING	EVENING
1¾ gallons	1 gallon

- Scrubbed buckets.
  Made chèvre from four gallons.

JULY 21

In my lap—a doe,
And in her lap—a harp;
She plays it with her fingers,
And kills me with her heart

—SA'ADIA IBN DANAAN,
FIFTEENTH-CENTURY GRANADA

The Hebrew and Arab poems about gazelles flourished in Andalusia between the thirteenth and fifteenth centuries with the blending there of Jewish, Ladino, Arab, and Spanish cultures. This was the so-called Golden Age of Hebrew literature. When people talk of this period in Spain, they speak of a literary and cultural "paradise." "Andalus," wrote the Palestinian poet Mahmoud Darwish, "might be here or there, or anywhere . . . Al-Andalus for me is the realization of the dream of the poem." Yet during that Golden Age poets still longed for another place, and the gazelle (or doe) stood in for that lost land. Then both Jews and Arabs were forced from Spain, and another land was lost.

Does it take exile to invent the whole concept of a land of milk and honey—a Zion, a paradise—a land some can enter and some cannot?

MORNING	EVENING
1¾ gallons	1 gallon

- Mucked barn. Limed outdoor paddock.
  Hung flypaper.
  Fed hay.

JULY 22

When I milk in the evening, I set a fan nearby to keep the flies and heat away. The does give less milk in the evening, but their milk seems frothier. Usually a four-inch head of sweet foam floats on top of the pail after milking. I'm convinced the idea of frothing milk for cappuccino originally came from hand milking a cow or goat. What else was a herder to do with a beautiful head of foam but cap his morning drink with it? Lately I've been spooning the froth into a drink I call "capraccino."

Capraccino

espresso
fresh milk froth
cajeta *(Mexican goat-milk caramel)*

1. Make the *cajeta* the day before as follows:
   In the morning pour a gallon of fresh goat milk into a wide pot and simmer. Ply the milk with two cups of sugar and stir.
   Leave the pot on low and stir every half hour or so. The *cajeta* is like the day: by evening it will begin to turn brown. When the milk and sugar caramelize to a gold sticky substance, it's done. Pour into a bowl and refrigerate.

2. Next evening call your goats to milk (most likely they'll call you). After milking carry milk directly into the house. Don't loiter; in half an hour the delicate froth will dissolve like ocean surf. Skim froth into a bowl and reserve.

3. Brew your espresso (black tea will work too).

4. Choose a squat, heavy-walled glass—not a cup, you want to *look* at it.

5. Pour espresso or tea.

6. Insinuate two spoonfuls of *cajeta* into the liquid—more if you like it sweet.

7. Top the rest of the glass with beautiful foam.

8. Sit in the shade with a view of the paddock.

9. Watch your goats head off to evening pasture.

10. Sip.

MORNING	EVENING
1¾ gallons	¾ gallon

- Trimmed hoofs.

JULY 23

Another scorching day, the sky a sheet of tin. I set the fan on high inside the doorway. The does lay sun-struck and panting in the shade. Everywhere the smell of urine and hay.

This evening the queen was dancey on the stand but I fended off her shins. It may have been just a fly landing on her pastern—she's been so good of late. We've grown to know each other on the stand. I would even hazard, there's trust.

Wherever the notion of paradise exists, so does the idea that it was lost. Paradise is always in the past, an unachievable land, an unattainable state. It elicits nostalgia and longing and sometimes bitterness. "A person who has not completely lost the memory of paradise, even though it is a faint one," says Eugene Ionesco, "will suffer endlessly." A taste of milk—and honey—forbidden on the lips.

When did Paradise disappear from earth? When couldn't you get there anymore in this body? When did it become either in the past or the future—but never now?

MORNING	EVENING
½ gallon	¾ gallon

- Scrubbed water trough.
  Made mozzarella from four gallons.

JULY 24

This evening a friend dropped by during milking; I made the mistake of letting him into the barn. He talked the entire time while I milked. The queen resented the distraction. She kicked the pail halfway through milking. I picked up the pail and started once more on her teats and my friend continued talking. *Blam,* down went the pail again. Hannah forces me into the moment and into silence. She reminds me of the Zen master who slaps his students, just to keep them present.

Yesterday I pulled two hundred garlic bulbs from the garden, bunched and hung them from the sunroom rafters. This evening when the breeze stirs, it brings a garlic breath throughout the house.

MORNING	EVENING
1¾ gallons	¼ gallon

- Ordered minerals.

JULY 26

When I sink into the rhythm of these days all this labor (the milking and cleaning and mucking and feeding kids) is pleasant, even in this heat. The end result is palpable: Milk. It's difficult labor but it's *my* labor and the best kind there is—that which directly feeds us. Gandhi believed that everyone—the banker, shopkeeper, poet—should spend at least a small part of his or her day producing the food they eat or the clothes they wear. "Bread labor," he and Tolstoy called it. In India, Gandhi urged everyone to spin their own homespun, that it would liberate both the country and the individual from oppression. He wrote: "If the poet spun half an hour daily his poetry would gain in richness."

These mornings I tend to believe in Gandhi's prescription; that one's own bread labor—labor that is not for hire, that doesn't turn into a commodity but feeds you—can enrich one's life and lead to a kind of liberation.

Maybe it's just the routine, the same objects in the same place (the wipes, the teat dip, the feed bucket, the scoop). The smallest change upsets the balance; and the repetition builds a kind of faith (milk stand, hoof trimmers, hay knife, stool). Rote is the nature of prayer. Incantation is repetition. Saying and doing the same thing over and over until *entranced*. Ritualizing the same physical motion with your body as Yogis do. My movements here on this milk stand are a kind of davening, a morning prayer with goat.

"All natural and necessary work is easy," wrote Gandhi. "Only it requires constant practice to become perfect, and it needs plodding. Ability to plod is Swaraj. It is yoga."

MORNING	EVENING
1¼ gallons	1 gallon

• Mucked barn.

JULY 29

Last night I woke to wind, a coolness in the house as if a stranger were moving through the halls. I heard him in the trees and in the garden; and suddenly the earth seemed lovely again and a new breeze sang through the screens. Dona slept, but Lola got up and went to the window and we stood together smelling wind and earth as if a great lever shifted somewhere in the universe. Stars spun overhead; and later back in bed I laid on an extra quilt against the cold and I could hear the goats across the lawn in the barn. Were they sniffing the new air as well? Did they sense that stranger too, moving in the cool of the garden—or was I the only one to feel him there?

In the morning on the milk stand I felt that cool against my back again, a breeze like someone's breath; and I felt a sudden indescribable joy. Hannah was on the stand. Lizzie watching. She leaned her head over the gate and sniffed my ear. Sometimes you make your own momentary paradise—it never lasts too long.

MORNING	EVENING
1¾ gallons	1 gallon

- Made chèvre.

JULY 30

Today again this lovely wind; the meadows plunge like waves. Trees toss their heads, the pasture turns to swells. This wind that comes midsummer, I don't know where it rises from or where it goes. We don't have enough words in English for our winds. *Boreas, zephyr, Santa Ana, Squamish, Chinook.* We need one here in New England. A local wind god. He comes this time of year, an ocean-faring breeze that brings hammered blue skies, clear mornings, fringed gentians, yellow hollyhocks, a constant seething in the dark. He makes these days seem so impermanent. A rock we cling to for a little while before we're scraped into the deep.

The milkings continue to pleasure. Nobody leaps the line. Before it was a chore but now a meditation, the Hebrew *Ameeda*. Silence the most important part. During my morning milkings no one talks. The animals like their routine. They won't tolerate noise or visitors or novelty. The only sounds a song or breath and the squirts of milk and the clank of the gate being closed. The calmer and more focused I become the calmer grow the goats. "What is important," wrote Basho, "is to keep mind high in the world of true understanding, then, returning to daily experience, seek therein the true and the beautiful."

We live in exile, not from Paradise but from the present. How often do we dwell there? How often does a wind bring us back?

MORNING	EVENING
1½ gallons	¾ gallon

AUGUST 1

Maybe paradise is all these things: a garden, an enclosed park, the memory of mother's milk or a golden age. Maybe the Garden is within or exists in the holiness of daily labor, the body making food for itself; or maybe it surrounds us every second if only we open our eyes.

Could it be that the *dheigh* at the root of the word *paradise* was, in fact, a dairy? A place *where people learned to milk other animals?*

MORNING	EVENING
1¼ gallons	1 gallon

- Made chèvre from four gallons.

AUGUST 2

We shall live in the shade of the
Graceful doe and, living there, shall be
Sustained. We shall walk through
Darkness by her light, with never-
Ending joy.

—DAVID ONKINERAH,
SIXTEENTH-CENTURY SALONIKA

The temperature dropped to 45 last night. The goats curled together in the barn, the kids piled in their pen. Everyone slept late. Even the queen didn't wake me this morning with her cries. I rose on my own, and outside the day hung gold and a kingfisher flashed over the pond. A hint of autumn braced the trees. When the goats came out they frisked in the sudden cool. They leaped and tagged around the picnic table. Even Hannah and Lizzie reared and butted. Hannah came to the fence and glanced across the wire with her come-hither stare. Her tail flicked back and forth and she moaned. I think my queen might be in early heat. After I milked her this morning she looked up at my face with amber eyes and licked my cheek. Today the queen loves me. Tomorrow, who knows? She might decide once more to kick the bucket.

MORNING	EVENING
1¼ gallons	¾ gallon

- Mucked barn.

PART III

Maturation

Deflation

THE SECOND WEEK OF AUGUST A CAUSTIC HEAT HUNG over the valley. Lizzie lay in the shade by herself and didn't graze with the others. Even in the grudging evening cool she stayed alone by the barn. A doe separated from her herd is a doe in distress, but we didn't know enough then to read the signs.

The next day her milk dropped to a trickle. Her ears hung flat and she kept stamping her left front foot. A day later we got her on the stand and slipped a thermometer in her rear. Her normal temperature was 102. Now the thermometer read 106.

We called Mary Beth and Dottie Cross. They had us inspect her eyes, her mouth, her hoofs (all seemed normal). We checked for mastitis with the California Mastitis Test Kit (negative). We checked for ketosis—a kind of hypoglycemia—by examining the color of her gums (they were red and healthy, not white). We checked for a stopped-up rumen by listening to her stomach (her rumen was working fine). Mary Beth suggested banamine—the equivalent of aspirin. Dottie Cross said a cold compress would lower her temperature, but that we needed penicillin *immediately.* Yet that first summer we had no penicillin on hand. We'd never needed it before.

In the barn Lizzie lay panting on her side. Flies sawed around her face. I filled a syringe with banamine, pinched the flesh around her shoulder into a shelf, and slipped the needle beneath her skin. Dona pressed a cold washcloth to Lizzie's face and neck. The other does came down to the barn and watched. Lizzie hung her head on Dona's knee.

The night never cooled. Crickets shirred in grass. Lizzie stared into space in the barn, fever in her eyes. Heat lightning quaked in the east.

The next day arrived steamy with August haze. I grabbed the milk pail and a hat. The herd milled by the fence yet Lizzie wasn't there. Neither was she in the barn. A goat doesn't go off by herself unless something is wrong. The scapegoat of the Old Testament is punished not by being driven into the wilderness but by being sent there *alone.*

I called for Lizzie but no response came back. I ran into the paddock and sprinted up the hill, shouted her name over and over, terrified about where she might be. I reached the top and flew across the flat. A harrowing howl came from the corner of the pasture. Lizzie stood against the fence, screaming. I called but she didn't turn to face me. *Lizzie,* I kept shouting, *what's wrong*?

She stamped a foot and screamed louder. When I finally reached her I put my hands on her back and held on to her neck and tried to calm her. She stared blindly ahead as if she couldn't see. I checked her flanks for wounds. Dona had heard my shouts by now and came running up the paddock. The does trotted behind—ears alert, tails cocked, looking all around with alarm.

Dona knelt and talked to Lizzie. Lizzie blubbered and howled. Her eyes seemed to show no life. It was not yet seven on a Sunday morning and the heat hung in metallic waves across the hills. We needed to call a vet *immediately*.

We helped Lizzie back to the barn. She stumbled and veered to one side like a drunk. The one good veterinary practice in the area that worked with goats was too far from our house. But that morning Mary Beth convinced the Granville vet to make the trip to our place. Mary Beth was on her way as well.

We put Lizzie in the barn. It was cooler there, and she couldn't wander away. The vet arrived at eleven, Mary Beth minutes after. The vet inspected Lizzie on the milk stand, shined a flashlight in her pupils, took her temperature and pulse, and listened to her lungs with a stethoscope. Lizzie stood listless in the stand and stamped her left front foot.

The vet closed one eye and peered down Lizzie's spine as if checking the trueness of a pool cue.

"Have you noticed," he asked, "that she's only turning to the left?"

We hadn't, but the difficulty of getting her back to the barn that morning was that she kept tacking to one side.

The vet's name was Brendan; his specialty was goats. He asked about the other does, the feed, the pasture, her rumen, our routine, how long she'd been ill. His diagnosis came remarkably fast. Lizzie had either listeriosis, an infection caused by the bacterium *Listeria monocytogenes,* or a parasite called the meningeal worm. The listeriosis would've likely been caused by bad grain. Yet Lizzie ate hardly any grain, and no other doe had fallen sick. Brendan was inclined to suspect the meningeal worm.

"A worm?" Dona asked.

Brendan nodded and gave us a quick tutorial on the natural history of the meningeal worm. *Parelaphostrongylus tenuis* is a hairlike parasitic nematode that lays its eggs in the brains of white-tailed deer. The eggs travel to the deer's lungs, where they're swallowed and excreted as larvae in their scat. Land snails then eat the deer scat and the worms become infective larvae within the snails. The white-tailed deer come along again and inadvertently eat the snails while browsing—and the cycle is repeated once more.

The arrangement works well for all involved, as the snails and white-tailed deer are unaffected by the presence of *P. tenuis* in their bodies. The problem occurs when another ruminant swallows the snail by mistake—a goat or sheep, a llama, alpaca, moose, or elk. When a goat ingests *P. tenuis* the infective larvae travel up her spinal cord and eat the nerves along the way, which cripples the goat. Eventually the larvae migrate through the brain stem, pass the blood-brain barrier, and enter the gray matter of the host; by that time the goat is often severely disabled or dead. If not caught immediately, the meningeal worm is fatal.

The vet finished and we all stood silent in the half-dark of the barn. I asked about the prognosis. Brendan said that with treatment, sometimes the animal came back fully, other times with permanent neurological damage. Yet often it was too late and the animal died. He couldn't say what the outcome would be for Lizzie.

Mary Beth began asking questions. Lizzie stamped her leg on the milk stand; she looked doped. I was heartbroken. The vision of her that morning beside the fence screaming and crippled kept playing over in my head. I excused myself and left the barn; it was all too overwhelming. A worm had entered our paradise—not a snake—and now it seemed there was little we could do.

Pathos

THAT NIGHT I READ EVERYTHING I COULD FIND ON THE meningeal worm. I read Smith and Sherman's *Goat Medicine,* D. G. Pugh's *Sheep and Goat Veterinary Care*. I found scientific abstracts online.

Once a goat ingests *P. tenuis* it takes five weeks for clinical disease to appear. That meant Lizzie must have swallowed a tiny land snail on a leaf or a blade of grass back in the rainy days of late June. Neurological disease results from tissue destruction caused by "randomly migrating larvae." The common clinical signs were loss of muscular coordination, stiffness, paralysis, head tilt, bent neck, blindness, weight loss, circling, depression, and death. The course of the disease, read *Goat Medicine,* ranges from death within days to loss of muscular coordination that lasts months or years. As for treatment, the vet manual didn't waste words: "Currently there is no known effective therapy for *P. tenuis*."

Despite the bleak outlook the vet laid out an aggressive treatment plan to save Lizzie's life. The next morning at dawn I prepared syringes and needles: 1¼ cc of banamine (to lower her fever), 1 cc ivermectin (to kill the worms), 6 cc oxytetracycline (to fight the infection), 3 cc thiamine (to boost her immune system), a needle of the steroid dexamethasone (to reduce inflammation).

In the barn that morning Lizzie looked dramatically worse. The neurological damage was now evident. Her spine had bowed to the left overnight; from above she looked saucer-shaped. Her head drooped farther down. It was as if, hour by hour, the worms were leaving lesions on her spine, crippling her bone by bone. Eventually *P. tenuis* would reach the blood-brain barrier and then her brain. It was now a race to see who'd get there first: the drugs or the worm.

Dona came out and milked, and afterward, while she soothed Lizzie on the milk stand, I shot Lizzie with five needles. She didn't complain once.

That week passed in a haze of heat and despair. The days came torrid and blanched, and Lizzie grew worse each day, her spine curving in on itself, a snake swallowing its tail. She was a large-framed goat, but always thin, all muscle, about 160 pounds. Now she looked skeletal. Her beautiful mahogany coat—flecked with burnt orange hairs and umber and black—seemed to hang off her frame now like a rug. Her face sagged. We fed her garlic; she'd always loved the bulbs and stalks, and garlic was said to be a good organic wormer. We didn't want to add the extra stress of drying her off just then, so we kept milking her morning and evening along with Hannah even though we couldn't keep her milk—it was poisonous with antibiotics and wormer. Each morning we helped her up on the stand (she couldn't leap anymore). I'd shoot her with needles in five different places, yet she was so bony and thin I soon ran out of places to pierce her.

On the third day she couldn't move at all to the right; her muscles just wouldn't work. It was as if she'd suffered a stroke. When she tried to rise and go out with the rest of the herd she'd stumble out of the barn and stagger in the only direction she could—to the left. She'd get stuck against the fence or a tree trunk; and there she'd stand moaning and bleating, trying to move herself to no avail. One of us would go out and physically turn her around and send her toward the herd. But she was like a boat with its rudder set only to the right. In another minute she'd drift off course and find herself moored against another tree.

The fourth day we had to lock her in the barn; it was the safest place for her. But soon even there her head got stuck in the iron manger. Her neck was curved so badly and she couldn't move her muscles to get herself out. We had to unscrew the manger from the wall.

All this time Hannah kept returning from pasture and calling down to the barn. Where was her sister Lizzie? It seemed she was trying to coax her out to graze. The sisters had never been separated before, and Lizzie's illness stressed Hannah too. She couldn't graze for more than ten minutes at a time without returning and calling to Lizzie. Why was her sister not coming to her call?

Of all the does, Lizzie was the hardest to see so reduced. Lizzie with the face stripes, the perfect milker and mother and protector of the herd who policed the barnyard at night and took up the rear when grazing, She was fading before our eyes.

Throughout that week I grew increasingly distraught. Why was I so affected by a sick goat? Was it because Lizzie had fed me for the last few months with her own milk—or that I'd fed her? Or that we had what the Kalapalo Indians of Brazil call *ifutisu,* a lack of shyness, that which we share with our house pets, our dogs and cats, a physical intimacy we rarely have with other humans?

The nature of empathy bewilders me, how we can feel one way about certain animals and the opposite about others; how we can inflict pain and death on some and shower love on others and feel more deeply for an animal than a fellow human. Do we reserve pity, as Aristotle says, only for those who suffer *undeserved misfortune*? Is that why it's easy to feel for a sick animal or an injured child, those who couldn't possibly have "deserved" their misfortune? Or is all empathy cultural, as Christians learn to weep over the Passion and Japanese over the *chushingura,* and Shia Muslims cry at the story of Imam Hussein's murder. Does one's culture, one's class, determine pathos, and is all empathy a secret kind of selfishness?

I started practicing the words: *We had to put her down*. How reasonable they sounded. There was a brutal comfort in them—*we had to put her down*—for how much more of this could the goat take? How much could *we* take?

I spoke often that week with Jennifer Lawrence. She and her husband, Melvin, ran a goat dairy a half hour away. Melvin was a third-generation farmer. He'd milked Jerseys alongside his father all his life, but just the year before had traded all his cows for goats. Sick animals were nothing new to the Lawrences. Jennifer had nursed countless ailing cows and goats back from the brink of death—and Melvin had shot the incurable ones. One Alpine doe was so sick she couldn't move or stand, and Jennifer had to put finely chopped hay deep inside her mouth day after day just to get her to eat. After a week Melvin wanted to euthanize the goat. Jennifer said no, she's not ready. She doesn't want to die. She said: *All she wants to do is be a goat*. She wouldn't let Melvin shoot the doe. Two weeks later the Alpine recovered. Today you wouldn't know a thing had ever been wrong.

Jennifer said over the phone, "You can't give up on an animal until it's given up on itself. You owe them that much. When she's ready to die, you'll know."

"How will I know?" I asked.

"You'll know," Jennifer repeated, and there was a pause on the line and she exhaled as if it was too obvious to say. "For one, she'll stop eating."

Mary Beth Bolduc once had a deathly ill doe, and her husband, concerned for that animal's suffering, was ready to put her down. But Mary Beth fed the goat back to health. Why was I so ready to give up on Lizzie, as Jennifer's and Mary Beth's husbands were? Lizzie was doing what she needed to do: being sick. It wasn't her distress I couldn't handle, but my own.

Days passed. The sun baked the valley. Chipmunks stayed under earth. At dusk, long-horned beetles followed the scent of fresh-cut wood to their wounds. The orioles were already migrating south.

Lizzie faded from day to day, a trace of her former self. She could hardly stand on her own.

You'll know when she's given up, Jennifer Lawrence said.

We didn't know yet, but soon it seemed we would.

Domestics

OUR NEIGHBORS KEPT A DOZEN SHEEP. DORSETS MOSTLY, castoffs no one else wanted who they fed and let run on plenty of pasture. The neighbors owned several hundred acres and the sheep's primary function was to keep the grass down in unused pastures. The neighbors cared about their animals—they kept horses and cattle too—but were laid-back about their fences: a few strands of rusted barbed wire, a locust post here and there bleached by weather, a gate a dog or coyote could simply step through. To protect their sheep they'd installed a llama with the flock. Llamas make good livestock-protection animals, and this llama towered seven feet over the sheep. He was white in front and brown behind and looked like an oddly shaped black-and-white cookie. We'd drive up the valley and see him a quarter mile up a hill, ever alert, tracking our car with his pointed periscope head attached to an impossibly long neck. If we got anywhere near him he'd pucker his thin lips and make an awful sucking sound, a warning he was getting ready to spit. Face spitting was one of his defenses, his powerful legs the other.

That summer the llama's flock began to disappear. No one noticed right away because the neighbors lived far from the sheep, who in summer required little care. But one morning a ewe's carcass lay in the field beside the road. Anyone driving up the valley could see it. The ewe had been eaten from the anus inward, and part of her intestines were gone but her head and legs still intact. The next day more of the carcass was consumed; then turkey vultures arrived. In a few days we had to roll the car windows for the rancid smell. Eventually the neighbors shoveled lime over the remains and covered the carcass with a tarp.

People blamed coyotes. They hunted in packs; and everyone in the valley agreed that once coyotes killed a sheep they'd kill again. About this, they weren't wrong.

The neighbors moved their sheep up the valley to a pasture with a barn the sheep could run to, but the fences there were just as poor. Coyotes struck again. More sheep disappeared, killed on the way to the barn.

By September, only one ewe and the ram and the llama were left in the flock. The llama had a haggard look. The ram never left his side. The ewe wore a doomed expression and would run and hide if anyone tried to come near. By the first frost, only the llama and ram were left; then, a week later, they disappeared as well. The neighbors searched the nearby woods. The llama and the ram couldn't be found—not even their bones. They'd vanished without a trace.

Rifle season arrived. The valley echoed with gunfire. Then blizzards came and snow entombed the earth. Winter was neither mild nor terribly harsh, but there were twenty-below nights and blinding snowstorms; and everyone by then had forgotten about the llama and the ram.

•

Animal domestication is often thought of as a symbiotic relationship. In exchange for food and protection, the goat or sheep, horse or llama forfeits their autonomy and independence. The most important decisions in their lives—when to eat, drink, breed, and where to walk (*if* to walk)—are dictated entirely by humans. While domestic cattle, chickens, goats, sheep, and pigs have done well as species in terms of numbers and distribution throughout the world, humans have benefited the most by their domestication. One look at the life of an average industrial steer or pig makes clear who is benefiting and who is not; it also underlines the definition of a domestic animal as one *bred in captivity for the purpose of subsistence or profit*.

Humans successfully domesticated only a relatively small handful of the world's animal species. Early Egyptians attempted to domesticate hyenas, antelopes, ibex, and gazelles. Indigenous Americans kept raccoons and bears for pets; Australian aborigines, wallabies and kangaroos. None survive today as viable domestic animals. What made the wolf (*Canis lupus*), the Bezoar goat (*Capra aegagrus*), the Urial sheep (*Ovis vignei*), the progenitor of the cow, the auroch (*Bos primigenius*), the Eurasian wild boar (*Sus scrofa*), and finally the horse (*Equus caballus*) successful candidates for domestication was a set of preconditions or "preadaptations" that lent themselves to human manipulation. These were all highly sociable animals that lived generally in mixed-sex groups with clear dominance hierarchies, and thus were relatively unaggressive; the animals knew how to back down in the face of an alpha male or female. They all had fairly wide-ranging diets and were easy to breed in captivity. Humans were able in effect to "talk" to them and even, at times, listen.

Goats and sheep were particularly good candidates for domestication. Ungulates who lived on the plains, like gazelles and deer, had hair-trigger flight responses in order to outrun predators they lived among. But goats and sheep, who lived in mountains, were not terribly swift at flight. Their survival depended less on eluding predators than on finding enough to eat. As such they were relatively unafraid of humans and their dogs. Humans could steal their kids or lambs and raise them as their own. They required only food and care and a modicum of protection.

Once animals became domesticated they began to change in ways that generally benefited man, not beast. Domesticated species as a whole developed less sensory awareness, larger stomachs, and smaller brains than their wild ancestors (for why did a domestic animal need a good brain anymore when others were thinking for him?). In the wolf, domestication led to arrested development, permanent adolescence, and a stunting of natural instincts. Some animals became in time unrecognizable behaviorally, and soon physically, from their wild ancestors. Domesticated animals became, in short, docile, fat, and dumb.

Back in the valley spring arrived the following year. The snow thinned in the woods. One morning a man who lived across the notch spotted a strange animal at the side of the road. The animal had eight legs and one head, but fled before the man got a close look. People started calling the beast "the octopus."

Another month passed; it was almost April now. This time the same man caught a better view. The animal was grazing near the edge of the road, and when it looked up he saw a periscope head staring at him. Beneath the animal's belly, a ram stood peering from under matted wool.

The neighbors who owned the sheep were apprised. They drove their truck across the notch and up the hollow, and there stood the llama and the ram side-by-side. All of us in the valley had assumed the coyotes had killed them or hunters or the winter snow or the lack of food or cover. But they'd survived the winter just fine all on their own—better perhaps than under human care.

The neighbors shook a bucket of grain and the llama and the ram came to the truck. With harnesses and tethers and a ramp, they loaded them and drove them back down the valley. This time the neighbors weren't taking chances. They put the llama and the ram inside a barn and closed the door. Yet that night, the llama and the ram escaped. They probably didn't think themselves any safer inside a barn than out, given their experience. What good was a fence if it only kept them in and nothing out?

The next morning, the neighbors found the two animals again and hauled them back in the truck. This time they put them in a barn stall they couldn't jump or kick down. After a few days the animals seemed to submit once more to their domestic situation.

In the valley we marveled over the llama's and ram's resources, their determination and grit—but that seemed partly to miss the point. Animal heroics are often misinterpreted acts of desperation. The llama and the ram wanted merely *to survive.* When we give domestic animals the freedom and physical space to express themselves we're often surprised at what they still can do despite millennia of human genetic manipulation. We're surprised because we expect the thing we've inculcated in them: dependency and degradation—the factory cow or pig who lives in her own waste. We're surprised by domestic animals' independence and dignity because so often we've taken that dignity away.

•

A week after the llama and the ram were brought back down the valley, the neighbors discovered an unsightly growth on the ram's testicles. How long it had been there, they didn't know, but this time the neighbors wanted to do right by the ram. They called in a vet; a diagnosis was pronounced. A tumor. Was it causing the ram any pain? It certainly didn't look good. Who knew what the ram would've wanted. He still walked alongside and under the llama—the two were inseparable. Yet it didn't really matter what he wanted. He'd come back from the wild and entered the domestic world again, where decisions were made for him; the decision was to operate.

Sheep are notoriously delicate animals, despite the tenacity the ram showed all winter. The vet went to work on him one April morning when the white trillium bloomed like napkins in the woods. The ram panicked. He began to bleed out. The last thing he saw before his heart thumped to a halt was the llama, his other half, a periscope staring down at him from the top of a fenced-in hill.

Other

LIZZIE BEGAN TO RALLY IN THE MIDDLE OF AUGUST. One morning she made it up to the milk stand on her own. I milked her and afterward Dona brushed her coat, and when we went to put her back through the gate, she stayed on the stand and looked up into our faces. We both noticed the recognition right away—a presence, something in her eyes that hadn't been there for weeks. Lizzie seemed all at once back with us; and though it took her a long time to recover, from that morning on we knew she was going to live.

For weeks her spinal muscles permitted her to turn only to the left; yet day by day she learned to deal with the disability. When she grazed with the herd she'd drift off to the left and find herself alone. To get back to the others she'd make an ever wider counterclockwise circle until she joined the herd again. *All she wanted was to be a goat*—and slowly her spine straightened and she grew stronger. Dona massaged her spinal column each day, and the bond between them grew intense. In the pasture the mahogany doe with the face stripes would lay her head completely in Dona's lap and close her eyes and they'd stay like that together for nearly an hour—woman and goat.

In two months, Lizzie was back to normal, save a loping gait she has to this day.

Late August, the woods began to thin. Crickets shirred in the dry grass. We finally found a buyer for Lizzie's spotted doelings—a woman who wanted goat companions for her Appaloosa mare. Spots with spots. As much as we hated to part with the kids, we didn't have room in the barn.

The last Saturday in August the woman and her husband arrived in a blue pickup. Goldenrod swayed in the breeze, the wild bergamot smelled of tea. Dona called the herd in from the pasture. Seconds later Hannah, Pie, Nisa, Penny, Eustace Tilley, and the spotted sisters spilled down the hill with hoots and moans. All but Lizzie, who stayed on the rise, ears pressed forward at the strangers. We called her again and she called back but came no farther.

Almost a year had passed since we'd picked up the four does from Mary Beth's farm, a year since they'd first arrived in our paddock with the apple trees. Now we were the ones giving up our goats, and it would go like this each year, new kids born in spring—four, then seven, then twelve—a new crop of bucklings and doelings. We'd feed them milk through the summer and three months later watch them go. If we were lucky we'd sell them all to good homes, even the bucklings. You can castrate a buckling and turn him into a wether, and he'll make a wonderful companion animal for people, horses, or sheep. Stick a bell on him and he becomes a "bellwether," the animal that leads the herd into the field (hence our English expression). But most bucklings are raised for meat and slaughtered anywhere from eight weeks to ten months old. Young, milk-fed *capretto* is meltingly tender. Older kids are barbecued or spitted and roasted whole, and still older ones braised, stewed, jerked, or curried. And this we understood well: that dairy comes with death. You can't eat an ice cream or a latte without killing animals. All those unwanted boy calves, lambs, and kids inevitably end up butchered.

The woman and her husband played with Lizzie's twins. The couple had visited earlier that summer and had chosen for them new names. Now the rest of the herd crowded around the newcomers—all but Lizzie, who stayed stubbornly on the hill. One of the spotted kids looked up the slope and called to her mother, and Lizzie called back. The kid climbed the hill, but Lizzie didn't budge. We were all watching now—Dona, the woman and her husband, even the other goats. The kid put her face up to Lizzie's and stayed there for a few seconds. Lizzie, still handicapped, made a brief head nod to her doeling. Then the kid turned and hoofed back down the hill.

Did Lizzie sense her kid was leaving? Was the doeling saying goodbye? The questions about animal cognition are endless—what do they know and how much and are they conscious or even *self*-conscious? We might never fully know, yet the longer I spent with our goats, the more complex and wondrous their emotional life seemed: their moods, desires, sensitivity, intelligence, attachments to place and one another, and us. But also the way they communicated messages with their bodies, voices, and eyes in ways I can't try to translate: their goat song. Lizzie and her kid were having a conversation—if only I had ears to understand.

"We need another and a wiser and perhaps more mystical concept of animals," the naturalist Henry Beston wrote. "In a world older and more complete than ours they moved finished and complete, gifted with extensions of the sense we have lost or never attained, living by voices we shall never hear.

They are not brethren, they are not underlings; they are other nations, caught with ourselves in the net of life and time."

Lizzie's kids were bundled into the blue pickup. The humans exchanged money and papers. Lizzie at last came down the hill and called to her twins. The other kids pressed their faces to the fence and called too. After the pickup left, Lola lay flat in the grass. Nisa and Pie and Hannah cudded under the bright sun, while Penny and Eustace Tilley grazed on the hill. Lizzie alone remained by the fence for another full hour. She stared down the driveway, high wind in her hair, looking at the place where her daughters last had been.

Terroir

There will be enough goats' milk
For your food,
For the food of your household
And maintenance for your
maidens.

—PROVERBS 27

THAT SUMMER I MADE CHEESE EVERY OTHER DAY. MOSTLY I made chèvre and sprinkled it with chives or summer savory or sometimes lavender blooms. Sometimes I'd roll a cake in ground pepper or—unsalted—mix the curds with cranberries and walnuts. In spring we ate chèvre with wilted watercress or dandelion greens, or a dollop on top of fried eggs and asparagus. In summer we ate chèvre on grilled eggplant and zucchini, in pasta, or with black beans, salsa, and chips. We ate *faisselle* with woodland berries soaked in maple syrup, or with peach slices when they came into season.

Our chèvre had little resemblance to the goat cheese one finds in a store. Mass-produced chèvre, wrapped in plastic or vacuum sealed, often comes from previously frozen curds or even powdered milk—and the milk is *always* pasteurized. Our chèvre had as much in common with store-bought as a sun-ripened tomato plucked from a vine in August resembles one grown under lights in February. No supermarket can get around the simple truth, says cheese expert Patrick Rance, "that goat cheese is a seasonal joy."

I made mozzarella, too, that first year. The cheese was firm and salted and slightly piquant, good for slicing, melting, or grilling on pizza. All summer breakfast was toast and thick slices of mozzarella. In August we lived out of the garden—tomatoes, basil, beans, fennel—and mozzarella from the goats. There *was* enough goat's milk for our food.

I was studying the cheese standards then: Pierre Androuet's *Complete Encyclopedia of French Cheese,* Patrick Rance's *Cheeses of the World,* Ricki Carroll's *Home Cheesemaking,* Jean-Claude Le Jaouen's *The Fabrication of Farmstead Goat Cheese,* Paul Kindstedt's *American Farmstead Cheese,* and a small newsletter from the Vermont cheesemaker Peter Dixon called *Farmstead Cheesemaking.*

I tried my hand at making other cheeses: a feta whose curd developed an off-putting salmon pink mold. An asiago, which never formed a rind (and tasted like a salted hockey puck). A provolone, which I didn't have the patience to age, but ate fresh. I did make sweet, delicious ricotta a few times from the whey. But a hard aged cheese, I learned, would take a lot more time and knowledge to achieve.

Every raw-milk cheese is an artifact of the land; it carries the imprint of the earth from which it came. A cheese—even a fresh chèvre—is never just a thing to put in your mouth. It's a living piece of geography. A sense of place.

Winemakers talk about the *terroir* of a particular wine, how a place's geology, drainage, soil, plants, and weather all contribute to a vintage. You can't create *terroir* artificially. It's the gift of a place, and what makes a pinot noir grown in one part of Burgundy taste different than one grown a kilometer away—let alone the same grape raised in Australia. *Terroir* is the DNA of a place. It translates roughly as the "taste of the soil."

To make a cheese you need a Mardi Gras of different life-forms—bacteria, fungi, yeasts, plants, mammals—all commingling in an age-old carnival. The Connecticut nun, cheesemaker, and scientist, Mother Noella Marcellino, discovered only a few years ago that dozens of different strains of one type of fungus—*Geotrichum candidum*—grew in one region of France alone. *G. candidum* is one of the first fungal growths that colonize the rind of an aging cheese. Mother Noella found that one farm in the Auvergne hosted a particular strain of *G. candidum* while another in the next valley hosted a different strain, and scores of other strains thrived elsewhere—in Normandy and the Alps. It was as if one type of unknown mushroom grew in one valley, another in the next, and hundreds of others all over the world—and each particular strain imparted a unique flavor to the cheese on which it grew. Such astonishing biodiversity on a microscopic level was a revelation to Mother Noella, and the entire cheese world. She confirmed in a lab what people had suspected for centuries: that *terroir* is found not only in the earth, but in the air.

What were the particular qualities of our cheese? What constituted its *terroir*? First our breed of goats—Nubians—lent the high butterfat and sweet taste to the milk. Then what the does were eating that day at pasture: the yarrow, thyme, wild bergamot, and clover in the orchard; the maple leaves and sweet vernal grass on Mason's Hill. All of these plants appeared as aromatic compounds—esters, aldehydes, alcohols, ketones—a few hours later in the milk and still later in the cheese. The stage of plant growth affected the cheese as well, as did the acidity of our soil, the washes of gravel, green schist, and quartz; the Northern Spy apples, which fell early to the earth; the invisible organisms in the air around our house and inside the cellar (where I eventually aged the cheese). Everything around us contributed to the taste of our *terroir*. And since the goats' milk changed from day to day, the cheese changed too, *in statu nascendi*. Our *terroir* was a moveable feast.

If small-scale farmstead cheesemaking seems a luxury today, we forget that farm cheese was once a staple in rural America. Only a few decades ago, before and just after World War II, thousands of American women milked a cow in the morning and evening. They left the milk out to clabber or soured it with store-bought rennet or sometimes vinegar or lemon juice. The curd was put in a cheesecloth or a wooden mold, or broken up into cottage cheese ("cottage" because it was made at home) or farmer cheese (because it was made on the farm); these were simple fresh white cheeses—salted and eaten the next day or days. Some made their own aged cheese as well. Both fresh and aged came from raw unpasteurized milk (from animals that ate grass). For centuries this was how people stored their surplus summer's milk, by turning it into cheese. For an aged cheese stored in a cellar—without refrigeration—can last for years.

Many of the older residents of our valley still recall the fresh cheeses their mothers or grandmothers made. Several of the farmhouses have whitewashed rooms in their cellars with rock or slab floors that betray the existence of a former milk or cheese room. Buried in the walls of our own basement lay a summer kitchen—a huge stone fireplace that had been plastered over by succeeding generations. I imagine that two hundred years ago, the family who lived in this farmhouse also made cheese, that they stored their milk down in the summer kitchen, which stayed cool all year round. (The town records show their family name was Herd, and back in England, their surname was once a job description—Herd for "herdsman.")

If today the concept of *terroir* seems foreign to Americans, we forget that people here once knew how place affected taste. "The cheeses of the granite hills and valleys of New England," noted a nineteenth-century traveler, "differ from those of the secondary soils of . . . northern New York, while the latter differ from those produced in the shales of . . . northern Pennsylvania; and they again are a different article from the cheeses made on the slaty clays of the Ohio Western Reserve." Granite, slate, shale, clay—we once knew the earth informed our food.

That first summer we were milking only two does, yet even with the limited supply we made enough cheese to eat year-round. We froze the chèvre curd and brought it out in winter; newly salted and herbed, it was vastly superior to anything we could purchase, but not the "seasonal joy" of a fresh *faisselle*. The cheesemaking was like farming; we did it when the season allowed. This was the traditional way, making hay when the sun shined and storing it for winter. It followed the natural cycle of the animals' lactation, which worked in concert with the bloom of grasses and leaves and slackened in the fall. In September we started drying off the goats. Just before the last leaves fell from the trees, we stopped making cheese.

People who tried our chèvre said they'd never tasted anything like it. They wondered why it tasted so different from what they'd bought in a store. We had to confess: it had nothing to do with our skill or lack thereof. Our fresh cheese was simply made from clean raw milk. As such, it couldn't be bought or sold anywhere in the United States. If we sold it we'd be put in jail. It was as if we were making not cheese, but moonshine.

Raw

ALTHOUGH WE COULD SELL OUR FRESH RAW MILK DIRECTLY from—and only from—our farmstead, selling our fresh raw-milk *cheese* was out of the question. No matter how healthy our goats, how virgin our pasture, how scrupulous our cheesemaking, if we sold or traded our chèvre we'd be breaking federal law. The U.S. Food and Drug Administration law Title 21 CFR Part 133 prohibits the sale of raw-milk cheese that hasn't been aged at least sixty days. Our chèvre and mozzarella weren't aged at all.

To pasteurize milk the liquid is heated to at least 161 degrees Fahrenheit and held there for fifteen seconds. The heat kills most of the bacteria that cause illness—*Escherichia coli, Listeria monocytogenes, Salmonella.* Yet it also destroys the nutrients in the milk, its enzymes and vitamins—not to mention its flavor.

Milk comes out of a mammal alive with microorganisms. The microbes exist to nourish and help the survival of the mammal's offspring. Some organisms, like the macrophages and T lymphocytes, aid the infant's immune system; others, like lactoferrin and lysozyme, kill harmful bacteria. The enzymes—

peroxidase, catalase, phosphotase, amylase, lipase, galactase—help digestion, while the oligosaccharides are indigestible and seem to exist solely to feed beneficial bacteria living inside the infant's stomach. All these compounds are found in raw milk—whether the milk of a cow, goat, horse, human, or whale. Pasteurization kills them all and turns the milk into a dead thing.

For thousands of years people believed fresh raw milk was a panacea. Hippocrates prescribed milk for people with tuberculosis. Arab physicians touted camel's milk. German and Russian physicians in the nineteenth century popularized the "milk cure," which was said to treat everything from liver disease to asthma. In the United States the Mayo Foundation (a forerunner to the clinic) promoted its own version of the milk cure, insisting that raw milk cured a plethora of ailments. What all these lactic enthusiasts shared was the belief in the powers of unpasteurized milk from a *healthy animal fed what she was meant to eat*—namely grass.

Yet things didn't always work out so well for the cow. As a way of cleaning up the wastes from beer and whisky making (and turning an extra dime), American distillery owners in the nineteenth century crammed dairy cows into cellars and bricked enclosures and fed them hot fermented distillery waste. The resulting milk, called swill or slop milk, was notably blue and often deadly and sold on the cheap to the poor. Some dairies added chalk or plaster of Paris to their milk. Once milk became transportable by train and then truck, milk traveled from farther afield, and city dwellers could no longer verify the cleanliness of the place their milk came from. Unsafe milk caused outbreaks of diphtheria, scarlet fever, typhoid fever, tuberculosis, brucellosis. It's no wonder that at the turn of the twentieth century the cry for clean milk was considered a moral cause.

Pasteurization was one method of assuring safe milk; another was strict inspection and certification of dairies. Each method had its advocates. But certification—a process of making sure the animals were healthy and the dairies spotless—lost out to the quicker fix: pasteurization. Pasteurization worked. People no longer died from drinking milk. Yet pasteurization often became an excuse for dairies to sell, not clean milk from healthy animals, but filthy milk from sick animals whose milk had been cooked clean of its impurities. Rather than rigorously certify raw-milk dairies—as is done in Europe today—it was less costly for the American dairy industry to simply zap their milk. Throughout the twentieth century, compulsory pasteurization laws in the United States expanded state by state, until it became nearly impossible for Americans to find anything but pasteurized—and effectively dead—milk.

Today in North America the typical industrial cow (organic or not) lives in a slurry of manure. She never walks on pasture or eats grass. She's fed what she was never intended to eat—high-energy grain. She will produce twice as much milk by eating grain instead of grass, but she'll become chronically sick from it. A diet of grain will lead to knotted guts, bloat, abscessed livers, ulcerated rumens, rotten hoofs, udder inflammation, shock, and eventually death. The average industrial milk cow lives less than five years. A cow allowed to eat grass on pasture can live fifteen or longer.

In a tiny operation like our own, there's no need to pasteurize the milk. We know beforehand if a doe is sick, and the quality of the milk is obvious because it sits right beneath our noses. Several states (like Vermont) recognize the relationship small farms have with their animals, and allow farmers to sell raw milk directly from their farmstead. The farther milk has to travel from the teat, the greater the chances it can degrade. If our own raw milk was trucked out of the valley and traveled a few hours and sat in traffic on a city street and then on a shelf somewhere in a store, we couldn't vouch for its safety. Not because of what happened here *in situ*, but what might've happened once it left the valley. All this argues for a local source: an animal and a farmer one actually knows.

The debate over raw versus pasteurized gets a lot of people up in arms. Unpasteurized milk is the birthright of most Europeans, and when you tell someone from France that in the States you can't buy a fresh raw-milk cheese, they look at you as if you've just profaned the Madonna. It confirms everything they suspected about American culture: that there is none—especially when it comes to the cultures inherent in milk.

The simple truth is that you can't make a top-quality cheese from pasteurized milk. Pasteurization kills over 99 percent of the milk's bacteria, including all the good, but not necessarily the bad, bacteria. Pasteurization incinerates the building blocks of a good cheese—the *lactobacillus* indigenous to the milk. It also destroys the aromatic esters—the monoterpenes and sesquiterpenes—from the plants the animal's been eating, which give raw-milk cheese its unique herbal flavors, its *terroir.*

Raw milk is a living galaxy under a microscope. Commercial cheesemakers today go to great lengths trying to repopulate this milky way once it has been destroyed through pasteurization. But nothing concocted in a lab can replicate the diversity of microorganisms found in raw milk; and nothing can replace the natural antibiotic compounds—the lactogens—that inhibit the growth of harmful bacteria. Since pasteurization kills these protective inhibitors, pasteurized milk may be, ironically, *less safe* than raw during and after cheesemaking.

As advocates of the milk cure surmised long ago, there's something resident in clean raw milk that's good for humans. All mammals, after all, grow and become healthy on unprocessed raw milk. Scientists surveyed fifteen thousand children across Europe in 2007 and found that those who drank raw milk were practically free from all allergies. Those who drank pasteurized were not.

I never used to think much about milk. I hardly touched the stuff. Pasteurized cow milk made me slightly ill. Aside from a splash in tea, I mostly avoided dairy. I didn't much care for cheese, not because of the taste, but how it made me feel after. The goats changed all that. Goat milk is a lot closer to human milk than cow milk. Its fat globules are smaller and easier to digest and more resemble those of human milk. People drank goat milk for thousands of years before they ever tried the milk of a cow, which might explain why so many humans are still lactose intolerant to cow milk, and not to goat.

That first summer drinking unpasteurized goat milk I never felt healthier in my life. I didn't fall sick once, or come down with a cold, and the petty allergies that had plagued me for years disappeared. Like the sick man in the Yiddish tale, I was cured by the milk of a goat. As Gandhi said: the goat proved a mother to me. Like both men, I took my milk the way it came for thousands of years: raw.

Transhumance

As soon as Lizzie could get around I belled the goats again each afternoon and we hiked up Mason's Hill. It was the end of August now, the leaves already crisp on the trees. I'd lie up in the little bluestem grass with a book as the goats browsed around me. The books never lasted long. After minutes, I'd put the pages aside. There was enough to read all around—the sky and clouds and leaves. Mostly I watched the goats.

I once read you could train goats to herd themselves with a bellwether, or lead goat, and they'd follow in a circular route and browse their way back home. For weeks I tried to get the herd to walk the woods on their own. I led them up Mason's Hill and while they nibbled leaves I snuck back to the house. Yet after a few minutes, they'd drift back down the hill. I couldn't persuade them to head into the woods on their own. Goats are creatures of open range and mountaintop; they like long vistas where they can see predators approach for miles. Perhaps the dense New England forest gave them pause. Or perhaps they never developed the confidence of a non-bottle-raised herd. Whatever the reason, they depended on a human herder.

Before I raised goats I entered the woods to hike or hunt; find birds, mushrooms, solitude, or cordwood. Each walk was a kind of inquiry—*What will I accomplish, what will I see?* Yet with the goats I went into the woods with no purpose other than to herd. I expected nothing. I brought along a walking stick, a pocketknife, a bell. I brought a hat, a flannel shirt for a pillow. I once brought a rifle but realized—all wrong. It changed everything about how I walked the woods. Sometimes I brought a book. Always pen and paper.

The walking stick was not for herding goats (they wouldn't respond to a stick). I used it to bend down branches or knock crabapples off their boughs. The bell was for calling the goats. Mine was hammered copper on a leather thong that I tied to a belt loop. The goats wore bells that came from around the world—bronze or copper, iron or brass; some had wooden clappers or washers hung on rusted wires. We fashioned collars from old men's belts augered with new holes. Each doe wore her own belted bell so we could tell who was lagging or missing by the tone. Hannah, the queen, sported the largest bell (made of brass), the kids tiny copper ones no larger than matchboxes. All the bells had different timbres and together made an atonal music—a tintinnabulation—those afternoons. We sounded like a herd of North Pole reindeer.

The women herders of Sweden, the *valkulla,* once clanged pots and pans on their first forays into the woods to frighten off bears and wolves. I rang my bell each time we entered the forest. I rang it not for the goats to follow (they would anyhow) but to alert whoever else was around: coyote, fisher, bobcat, fox, bear, and that other predatory animal: humans.

The pocketknife was for slicing apples, or cutting free leather collars should two does get their heads stuck in one, as happened once when Nisa and Pie reached for a pile of acorns and came up with the same belt garroting both their necks. They nearly choked themselves fighting to get free. I had to cut through the hard leather and throw away the straps.

Late August, the pasture grass turned pale and lost what few nutrients it once contained. So each afternoon we roamed the woods in search of moosewood and honeysuckle and the fat spears of yellowing ash. We avoided low wet spots and cul-de-sacs with bad sightlines. I kept the goats away from the marshy banks of the brook. Most afternoons I moored myself on a rock and became the anchor around which all the does drifted. Each nodded off in her own direction. If they meandered out of sight I clanged my bell or sang them in and they swam back through the shadows of the trees as if lured by fishing line.

Herding is a menial task but also, historically, a prophetic calling. The shepherd-king reaches back long before Christ—the Good Shepherd—and predates all the herder-prophets of the Old Testament: Moses and Joseph, David and Amos. Perhaps the motif arose with Dammuzi, the Sumerian shepherd god, or maybe with Krishna, the Hindu shepherd god. Wherever it began, the image of the hero who leads his flocks in the fields and protects them from the wild lies buried in ancient human phylogeny.

The poetic muses came to Hesiod while he tended flocks on Mount Helicon. Moses walked his goats and sheep in Midian when the Burning Bush spoke to him. Shepherds first received word of Christ's birth; and the shepherd Muhammad heard the words of God in the wilderness. *No man becomes a prophet,* he later wrote, *who was not first a shepherd.*

Herding is an impoverished occupation, a job often relegated to children, the elderly, the slave or exile (Saint Patrick was a shepherd slave). Today the poorest people in the most impoverished nations subsist as herders of sheep and goats. So why the enduring myths? Why did God speak to shepherds and not, say, cobblers or dry-goods salesmen? Was it because shepherds lived apart, on land too dry, steep, or poor for other humans; or because they had all day to both dream and stay awake, and their hours were spent alone, in silence, watching animals, weather, and wind; and their minds could wander like their sheep and goats?

As long as there were shepherds, they migrated with the seasons. In summer they brought their herds to the high country where the grass was coming green. In winter they brought them back to the lowlands or river valleys to pasture them or feed them stored fodder. The system of moving animals seasonally to better grazing is called "transhumance," from *trans* for "across" and *humus* for "soil." *Across the soil.* Transhumance is ancient; the animal tracks it followed date back in some places to prehistoric times. Transhumance still occurs today in almost every continent on earth. In the Swiss Alps it's called the *Alpaufzug,* in the Chilean Andes, the *veranada,* in the Swedish north the *buforing*. In the Hindu Kush, in Kenya, in the Pamirs and Peru, the animals go up the valleys in spring like rivers running in reverse. All summer the herds stay up in the high pastures—the *alpage,* the *seter,* the *jailoo,* the *estive,* and *son.* It's often a bleak and lonely business for the herders. The days last long and the work is tough. But every account of transhumance, from today's Pakistan to the nineteenth-century Scottish sheilings, mentions the beauty and magic of living on mountains with herds. The Basque shepherds (all men)—who last century bunked together during their summer transhumance—bragged about the splendor of the Pyrenees and the purity of the mountain cheese they made up there. The Swedish herders (all women)—who last century walked their cows and goats to the remote spruce forests each summer—developed special songs for their herds. The women used a vocal technique called *kulning* that their animals were said to understand. When the *valkulla* returned to their villages in the fall, they hung up their herding bells and refused to sing their *kulning* songs back home. *Kulning* was the language of their summer transhumance, one meant for communion with other animals, and not with men.

In Western Europe, transhumance began to fade in the last few centuries and nearly vanished after World War II. New political realities (and borders), factory farming, rural depopulation, and the spread of rail and car made it impractical (or unnecessary) to move herd and household to the mountains for a whole summer. But the beauty of transhumance was that it worked in balance with the land, that herders followed the natural cycle of the summer bloom across the earth. The transhumant system gave lowland pastures a rest from overgrazing. By the time the herds returned to their valley farms in fall, they were coming home to restored pastures.

On my daily walks in Vermont I tried to incorporate the wisdom of transhumance. Each day I left the worn-out low-lying pastures and headed for higher ground. We walked away from home—from parasites and manure—and sought wilder earth. A lactating doe requires about eight pounds of dry matter a day. On our daily walks my goats ate far less than that, but the woods gave them a little of what they needed—wild greens rich in minerals and carotene. The walks gave me what I needed too.

Only a few decades ago—before they shipped their cattle on trucks—the transhumant herders of the high Spanish sierra walked their Avileña cattle down to the plains of Estremadura in early spring. The journey took several days, and hired herders did the job, yet the village men always went along too. When an anthropologist asked the men of one village why they walked their herds if they didn't have to, they made all sorts of excuses (the cattle were nervous; the herders needed help). Finally they all confessed: they walked their cattle because "we like doing it."

We like doing it. And I liked herding my goats, and people in cities like walking their Yorkies and pugs. There's something in the rhythm of walking animals—*andante, lento, corrente*—the companionable pace, the striking out into the world, the earth alive around us as we walk.

The Quaker range analyst Jim Corbett used to walk his goats into the Sonoran Desert of New Mexico for weeks and live off what the land and his goats provided. Corbett believed that with just a few milk goats one could walk away from the world and find "a peaceable kingdom." He believed that living a pastoral life offered a deeper understanding of the world, a way to live closer to the earth. "Goatwalking," he wrote, "reenacts the history of the prophetic faith . . . It's a way to be at home in wildlands. Living on milk and wild foods . . . It is also a form of errantry . . . in the sense of sailing out beyond society's established ways, to live according to one's inner leadings."

Those late summer afternoons wandering up the mountain, I entered a wiser world than the one I occupied each day. My human concerns slipped away, the house, the phone, work—all my bipedal obsessions. The goats walked at a meandering clip, less than a mile each hour. The tips of the maple leaves had turned blood red, and blue jays flitted through the bosk.

Books are like little forests, the philosopher Ortega y Gasset once said, each with its own natural history. But the forest was a book too. I entered with the goats on page one and lost myself leaf by leaf. Our path climbed through a text of birch and beech. I learned my landscape twig by twig.

Each afternoon I tried to lose myself up there. I tried to listen and watch. Beneath the bark of every tree was a layer called the *liber,* "the book." The Old English word for "book" and beech tree is the same: *bōc,* a plank of wood—something to read. Moses while walking his flocks saw an astonishing thing, a bush radiating voice, a talking tree. A Bedouin herder stumbled on the Dead Sea Scrolls while walking his herd of sheep. What texts could I find in my forest? The holy scrolls of oaks and ash etched inside with the histories of themselves? A library of talking trees?

I walked away each afternoon expecting nothing—and thus gained everything. The boy in the Yiddish tale went on transhumance. Instead of herding his goat, she herded him. "To wander" is the Taoist code word for "becoming ecstatic." At Passover Seders I'd always heard the refrain: *My father was a wanderer in the land of Aramea.* What I didn't know then was that he wandered there with goats.

Predation

A WEEK OF WINDY AUGUST DAYS ARRIVED AND THE farmers in the valley took to their fields; it was time to gather hay for the winter. Since we had no fields back then, nor equipment to make hay with, we drove across the mountain to our source. The Mattison brothers in New York State mowed several hillside meadows. We bought fresh bales off their wagon—sage green second-cut hay full of dried leaves and beautiful red clover buds. We needed three hundred bales to get us through the winter. It took five trips, over the course of a weekend, to load and haul the bales across the mountain and stack them inside our garage and a neighbor's barn. Bales were much cheaper back then ($2.25 off the wagon; more once they'd been stored inside a barn). The whole year's hay cost $730.

The mornings turned misty in September. Cinnabar leaves glowed on the still-green lawns. We gathered in wood as well, five cords for the winter. We split and stacked row upon row for weeks. Like the goats we depended on dry, pithy matter:

the biomass would keep us warm—just as roughage would heat the does on freezing nights.

September 9, a crescent moon pulled above the house. A frost was settling across the lawn. Dona was away, teaching for the night. I had just built a fire in the woodstove when Lola burst into howls. She scrambled to the back door, hair bristling, and raced into the dark. I followed and saw: a coyote lurked by the paddock. Another yipped from Mason's Hill. Lola stopped midway across the lawn and let loose an unearthly howl. The coyote halted. The other fell silent on the hill. Lola had the sense not to go nearer; she was no match for a coyote (let alone two or three). I shouted to scare them off and heard the crunch of leaves as they fled. Lola shot after them up Mason's Hill.

I ran to the barn to check the goats. They bunched together by the fence, alert, ears up, eyes riveted on the woods. Lizzie stood hard by the fence where the coyote had been. If Lola hadn't alerted me in time, would the coyotes have leaped the welded wire and gotten inside with the goats?

Lola came back from the hill after several minutes. I flooded the yard with lights and called her into the house. I dug a .35 Marlin from the closet, along with some rounds and a high-powered flashlight, and took them upstairs to the bedroom, where the window gave a clear view of the barn. The goats appeared in the sallow bore of the flashlight. Twelve phosphorescent eyes, like LED screens, shined back from the dark. If the coyotes returned, at least now I'd be prepared.

All late summer we'd heard coyotes at dusk, their high yipping chorus rolling off Bennetts Ridge. Their songs had increased each evening as fall approached, and sometimes a deeper, more resonant howl resounded beneath the rest: the adult male joining in (though some in the valley believed he was a wolf).

Heretofore we hadn't been concerned about the coyotes. I saw their tracks all the time in winter snow. They always transected Mason's Hill and headed east by northeast. They never came near the barn. Even if they did, our fences were new and tight, and the does spent most nights inside. We slept only a hundred feet away and would hear any commotion, and Lola would sound the alarm if it came to that. Yet now I wasn't so confident. What were the coyotes doing by our barn if not sizing up our goats? Juvenile coyotes in the Northeast disperse from their home range in early fall and try to establish new territories for themselves. They seek any opportunity they can find. Since our goats were new in the area, and this was their first September, perhaps they were precisely the type of opportunity the young coyotes were looking for.

Back in the house I plugged into a search engine the words *goat* and *coyote* and *predation*. Web page after page flashed photographs of coyote-killed goats. Range goats with udders eaten away or heads chewed off. A Boer goat with half its face missing. How high a fence could a coyote leap? Some said five feet, others six. It didn't matter how high the fence was, a coyote could always dig *under.*

I pulled on boots and walked back into the night. A low fog nosed Mason's Hill. I lured the goats into the barn with a shake of the grain bucket. I had to fight Lizzie into the door. The does hadn't been locked inside since the night they first arrived. I shut the light and latched the door. They'd be safer inside at least for the night.

I slept poorly that night. I kept seeing the goat with his head chewed off. Dona returned after midnight, and in the morning milked Hannah and Lizzie. I stumbled outside with the dog. Lola made a beeline for the fence where the coyote had been. (Suddenly the fencing seemed so inadequate.) Lola sniffed intently at the grass and leaves, moving with the scent. Ten feet from the barn she froze and stood with her nose fixed to the ground. A coyote scat lay in the grass; it was the size of a sausage link. I grabbed a stick and broke it apart to see what the coyote had been eating (apples, the most abundant food that time of year). I called Dona over and we stood a moment staring at the scat in distress. It was no casual dropping left in such a prominent place right beside the barn. The feces was a calling card, a message from a coyote who felt particularly at home in our backyard. It was meant not for us but for Lola. *You might think you own these goats,* it said, *but now we do.*

Lola squatted over the turd—and peed.

Years earlier, on a trip to the Lamar Valley in Wyoming, I saw a coyote kill an elk calf. I was in Yellowstone one morning as the sun rose over Soda Butte Creek. The coyote lay crouched beside a road. She was trying to hide among sage. Small, dirty blond, with an upturned pointed muzzle, she stared at an elk cow and her newborn calf a few yards away. Her golden eye barely blinked.

I'd pulled off the road with two biologists that spring morning; they were studying the impact of the recently reintroduced wolves on the local coyote population. Within seconds we all had our scopes and binoculars trained on the hiding coyote. She paid us little attention. Her mate watched from a bluff on the opposite side of the road. Their pups lay hidden in a nearby den. The biologists had been monitoring the pair for months.

The elk had delivered sometime in the night beside the road and the rest of her herd had since moved on, leaving her alone with her calf. The coyote's timing was perfect. When the mother wandered away for just a second, the coyote crouched and darted, stabbed and wrenched the calf's neck, and dragged the carcass away. The elk cow raced back and lowered her head, but it was too late; her calf was already dead. She bugled and stamped while the coyote hid beneath a bush. It was only a matter of time before the cow would wander away.

For the next hour we watched dispassionately while the coyote feasted. Each time she dipped into the carcass the fur around her muzzle came back redder, as if with cherry paint. The biologists said the elk cow was probably a first-time mother, that she'd birthed in a poor spot—so close to the coyote den (and road)—and that she'd not make the same mistake again. She moaned disconsolately as the coyote feasted. She'd return to the kill site, sniff the ground, and moan again. It was a sad sight, but this was the way the world worked. Grass turned into flesh and flesh to meat. Matter traded between forms. How you made your living depended on what you were given at birth: a stomach to consume grass or teeth to tear flesh. There was certainly nothing we humans could do at the side of the road except, of course, not *be* there.

One evening later that week I hiked up a scarp and scanned the Lamar Valley for wolves. Dusk was nearing. The road lay a few hundred feet below, an asphalt rill in shadow. In the binoculars I picked up a lone coyote about a mile distant standing on a sunlit ridge. She'd spotted me instantly and stared in my direction. I glassed the valley again. Some bison grazed miles to the east. When I turned, the lone coyote was clocking toward me at a steady trot.

I'd always admired the adaptability of coyotes, how when opportunity arose they seized it. To avoid a strenuous hunt coyotes will scare rabbits into passing traffic and lure human picnickers away from their lunch. In captivity they've learned to unlock cages by observing their human captors.

The lone coyote disappeared in a dip and reappeared on a closer rise. The biologists had loaned me a can of pepper spray in the event of a grizzly attack, but that evening I'd left the can in the car. The coyote was most likely just curious, just seeing if I was an opportunity (coyote attacks on humans are extremely rare). Yet standing alone on that ridge as the sun was going down, I felt exposed. I started back to the road. When I turned a moment later, the coyote was zeroing in; I didn't need the binoculars anymore; she was advancing at a lope. We were having the conversation that predators have with prey all the time—the testing, signaling, stotting—all part of the game both sides in the wild know so well, and why, in a place like the Lamar Valley, predator and prey can live side by side. Yet I wasn't from those wilds. I picked up a few rocks—and hurried quickly to the safety of the road.

That Yellowstone coyote was a western coyote—slight and wiry, about thirty pounds. The ones in our backyard in Vermont were the eastern subspecies, nearly twice the size and more likely to hunt in packs and take down larger prey, like white-tailed deer. Genetically and behaviorally, our coyotes somewhat resembled wolves—or a cross between the two. That morning, picking apart coyote scat beside our barn, I thought of the Yellowstone elk, and the neighbors' sheep down the valley, and all the understanding I'd nurtured for coyotes over the years flew instantly out the door. Class determines consciousness, Karl Marx observed; and now that I'd become a pastoralist, a keeper of livestock, hadn't I lost the luxury of appreciating all forms of life—especially those who might devalue my stock (coyote, bobcat, bear, meningeal worm)? Weren't coyotes now my avowed foe?

I walked the fence line later that morning. I stuck small boulders in gaps between fence and ground, ran barbed wire from tree to tree where the fence rode low, chainsawed felled logs that might give a leg up to a coyote. Then I called Melvin Lawrence, the dairy farmer. Surely he'd lend a voice of reason. For decades he'd raised Jerseys, and now dairy goats, in an area rife with coyotes. When I told him about the scat in front of the barn he was quiet for a long time on the phone. Then he said: "Brad, there's no compromising with coyotes. You're going to have to kill them."

Melvin gave me the number of a trapper, a woman who lured coyotes with a rabbit distress call—then shot them. Melvin said she was very good at her job. He offered to come by that evening to assess the situation. I told him I'd cook dinner. Before he hung up he said, "I'll bring my rifle and lights."

We locked the goats in at sunset. Melvin showed up after dark. By the time we arranged our gear—Melvin with his 7-gauge, me with the Marlin—a parchment moon floated above the house. We trudged up Mason's Hill and thrashed about in the woods for a long time. We stopped often to look and listen; our flashlight beams cut across the forest floor. I knew with all that commotion we'd see nothing, and Melvin seemed to sense it too.

What did we see that night? Tree trunks in lamplight, purple leaves plastered to the earth. Five deer raised their heads in a field, and green eye-shine flared from the dark. We saw the dropping moon enflame a meadow, and dew draped in webs across the grass. We saw not one coyote; they kept silent all night long. Back at the house, Melvin seemed not at all disappointed. I was secretly relieved.

Scatology

I SLEPT THOSE NIGHTS WITH THE MARLIN BESIDE THE BED, the window open a crack. We locked the goats in the barn each night at sunset. They didn't like losing the freedom to come and go, especially on dry, balmy nights when the does liked to sleep beneath the stars. Lizzie protested the most. I had to entice her into the barn at dusk with pretzels or raisins. Even with them closed in, I woke three or four times in the night while Dona snoozed, and poked my head into the pitch and listened with cupped ears. Was any sound by the barn, the woods? I'd light up the paddock with the high-powered flashlight and run the beam along Mason's Hill. I expected orange eye-shine, a coyote in the bluestem grass. Lola would join me at the window, muzzle stuck into the crisp, nostrils sucking in great drafts of air, decoding chemicals on the wind. Animal, vegetable, mineral. I relied on her nose to tell me who was there.

Some nights we woke to howls and Lola exploded into barks and rushed the window and I would too, or Dona, and we'd stand and listen and judge the distance from where the howls came to the barn. Dog and humans—the hairs rose on all our necks. Lola would throw her head back and howl, and then it would be over and silent, the night more alive and mysterious than before.

Everyone in the valley that fall saw coyotes crossing roads or walking in fields. Everyone had an opinion about what to do. The trapper wanted to call them in. A neighbor volunteered her son to shoot them. Another wanted to "mount fur" on his living room wall. Yet after my initial scare I began to think more sensibly about the coyotes. Surely there were other options aside from killing. We could keep locking the goats in at night. A guard animal might work—a donkey or a llama (though, based on the llama's performance down the valley, I was skeptical). There were livestock protection dogs, the Great Pyrenees, the akbash, the komondor, each bred specifically to protect sheep. We could leave a light on by the barn at night or a radio (the sound of a human voice was said to deter coyotes). There was evidence, too, that killing coyotes could make the problem worse. Since female coyotes can control the number of pups they have per litter, a population under siege tends to swell its numbers—producing even more juvenile coyotes.

All this took time to sink in—the light, the radio—yet I wanted immediately to let the coyotes know our goats were off-limits. I wanted to send a message, just as they'd sent one to us with their scat. So after that night of walking with Melvin Lawrence, I climbed Mason's Hill with the dog. Halfway up I asked in an excited voice:

"*Lola. Where are the coyotes*?"

She raised her snout and sniffed the air to the east and west. She'd known the word *coyote* since a pup, since we started using it in response to their howls. Now the flaps of her muzzle sucked in and puffed out. She lifted a front leg and pointed—then took off into the woods.

She traveled at a steady lope and I followed. The ferns had all died back and liver brown leaves freckled the earth. Sometimes Lola sniffed a low twig or the air, then continued steadily up the slope. Just as I was starting to lose faith, she came to a balsam thicket and froze and hung her muzzle over one spot. I caught up and saw a fresh coyote scat on the ground. Lola had taken me to the coyotes! I lavished her with praise. She looked up and panted. Then she squatted near the scat and peed. I added my own scent, sending the message back to the coyotes: *We're here too.*

Each morning for the next few weeks we tracked the coyotes in this manner. Lola would leave her sign and I'd leave mine. It must have been tremendously rewarding for the dog. For years we'd walked the woods each day, always on my terms, while Lola sniffed deliriously at every pert scent (deer, coyote, raccoon, mink). She knew exactly who'd passed in the night (turkey, squirrel, possum, weasel, vole); she'd shoot off by herself and return with the exhilarating news (porcupine, chipmunk, fisher, bobcat, bear!). But I hadn't been listening to what she had to say, and now I paid attention as she led. That first morning when she found the coyote scat and I praised her wildly she looked at me, tongue out, as if to say: *Finally, you get it. This is the real news. This is the shit!*

After a week of our patrols no more fresh coyote scat appeared in the woods—nor down by the barn or on Mason's Hill. Had we really scared the coyotes off? For the short run, perhaps. Or maybe they just became more careful about where they left their sign. To know for certain where they were heading, I had to wait for the first snow to fall. Then their prints would tell me the whole story.

Prints

WE DRIED OFF HANNAH AND LIZZIE IN OCTOBER. Their lactation had steadily slackened since August, when we started milking them only once a day. We could have milked them throughout the fall and winter, but we wanted to give the does a rest; we wanted to give *ourselves* a rest too. We'd made enough cheese to last the winter, and the prospect of milking at dawn in a frozen barn wasn't appealing. All of us would have a hiatus for the next seven months.

It took a few weeks to dry off Hannah and Lizzie. We milked them every other day, then every third day, then the fourth and fifth. Although their udders initially swelled with milk, the unemptied liquid was soon reabsorbed into their bodies. October 12 we milked them for the last time that year. By then the does were showing signs of heat. Soon it would be time to breed Hannah and Lizzie again—and Pie and Nisa for their first time.

The nights turned brisk in the valley. The coyotes bayed each twilight. We got to know their calls. One in particular, a high-pitched plaintive howl like a rooster's crow—*ro-ro-rooo.* She called each night from the field across the brook. I imagined her the adult female of the pack, because each night after her howl, the rest of the packlings joined in and the hills erupted with yips and barks. Wave after wave, a roll call echoed up the valley. *I'm here, I'm here, I'm here.* And all the dogs up and down the road responded with barks and howls, while the goats stared out the window of their barn.

One November morning, we woke to a painted world. Snow encaged each branch and limb. Lola was already out the door, a black streak turning figure eights across the lawn. When I asked, *Where are the coyotes*? she went stiff, then broke through snow up Mason's Hill.

The woods that morning looked rearranged. The birches bent in white arabesques, limbs scrolled in plaster casts. The last leaves on the beeches hung like metaled gold dusted with confectioner's sugar. Every branch articulated against gray sky.

We found heart-shaped deer prints, the prints of a snowshoe hare. Lola stuck her muzzle in each step and snuffled. Halfway up the hill she stopped. Her tail went up. In the snow lay what I'd been awaiting for months: coyote tracks.

The prints of a coyote resemble a domestic dog's, but dogs create a sloppy track where coyotes' prints are neat, with the two front toenails twinned close together. Coyotes also walk directly in their own footsteps, front and hind, in what's called "direct register." The prints we found that morning were tight and registered directly; they likely told the story of one coyote passing through the woods. But they may have told another story too. Coyotes can step precisely in the paw prints of their pack mates. While hunting in a group three or four family members can choreograph their movements through snow so as to appear to someone following their trail as one fluid animal. The trick is remarkable. Sometimes I've tracked a set of prints imagining a lone coyote only to have the prints divide into another pair and then another. A single line blossoming into a chorale. One animal multiplying to three.

We followed the coyote's track. Lola trailed behind inhaling each print. The coyote was moving up the mountain in a lope, its usual traveling gait. The prints seemed a little large; I decided it was a he—though I really couldn't know. He struck through a low thicket then into a grove of silver beech, out into open wood, on top of a downed maple—balanced there for several steps—then leaped back down to the earth. What was he doing hours earlier in the woods? He hadn't urinated yet or left his scat; he hadn't posted scent. He hadn't wavered in his course or slowed his pace. Yet now another trail intersected his: a squirrel's prints laid a little earlier, front and hind feet visible. The coyote had paused a moment to sniff the squirrel's track before heading on.

We continued too. The cuneiform kept coming, the fonts formed perfectly in snow, a sentence unspooling with no end in sight. What was the line saying? *This way . . . this way?* . . . a run-on that kept reading. I was no longer looking up but only down. The white of the woods was blinding. I was completely focused on dark dots. I looked up and felt dizzy. The woods seemed suddenly strange. I didn't recognize the dip or swale or glade mantled in its mattress of snow. The woods had suddenly defamiliarized themselves.

My heart raced. I hadn't realized we'd been climbing. Snow puffed from birches. Lola waited. A raven croaked in the chiaroscuro sky.

The place grew slowly familiar—the rise, the copse, the balsam thicket. This was the hollow Lola had led me up all fall, where we tracked coyotes. The sentence went there now. Lola ducked into the wall of balsams. I bent and followed inside.

We tunneled through a turnstile of pointed limbs, and out the other end the woods spread open again. No grapes hung in clusters, no honey dripped from trees, but I found myself emerged through a different divide, a paradise of two worlds wed together, an alphabet on the page and on the land—a literature of earth and woods.

The sky had no color. The earth had no color. Even the trees vanished under armatures of snow. It seemed I was chasing a narrative across a page, the story of this coyote and what he was after, a single thread among many in the woods. I followed the line intently. I wanted to know how it would end. Every predator's trail is a murder mystery, not a whodunit but *who was done*. How much do murder mysteries engage this old story? Why do we lust to see the kill at the end of the tale?

We went on. The dog, the man, the only dark objects in the whitescape. Two black figures scanning indentations in snow. The coyote slowed his pace; he stepped now in a double register, paws close together—almost overlapping. Had he heard something in the trees? A squirrel, a mouse? Was he listening for a rabbit? On a punky birch stub he left his mark for the first time in the area. Urine. I could see the spot. Two lemon drips: a colon. Lola took a long sniff, then hunched nearby and pushed out a tiny ball of stool: *exclamation point!*

This reading was all new to me, a second language. Real trackers scan a trail and make a midrash out of it. Kalahari Bushmen can read animals' emotions and moods in the tracks they find. They can describe copulation patterns of nocturnal animals they never see by day; or analyze an acre of moving eland and limn each individual and what he was doing and why, as if picking apart characters in *War and Peace*.

It started now to snow. The coyote was loping again back in a direct register, one paw print every two feet. I thought I should turn back; a coyote's range is large and one can trot for hours. What if his trail went on ad infinitum? What if the story had no end? Why are we so unsatisfied by tales that don't conclude, that have no gun, no knife, no corpse, that leave us hanging? What if this sentence just . . . . . !!! How much does our following words across a page engage the old neural pathways, and recapitulate the need to follow game and find . . . the food?

The snow was threading harder now, the sky emptying its gray. It was time to head back home, but the prints kept urging me on; the story wasn't over. I've seen beautiful things in snow. Circles of melted ice where a coyote slept balled beneath a fir. The wing drags of a turkey tom trying to impress a mate. The place where he leaped on her, the place where they mated, and where he leaped off again. A bobcat stealing someone else's frozen cache. So many stories each hour, each day, and I could barely follow this one coyote tale.

The tracks were filling now with flakes. A whiteout erasing type. A snowshoe hare crossed the coyote's trail. She must have arrived later. Her prints looked fresh and eager. I veered and followed them for a few steps. The tracks looked so alive, the fore and hind feet registering each tiny toenail. She paused and nibbled at a birch sucker, the twig freshly incised with her teeth; and just beyond she left a few tan pellets. I followed the confirmation of her leaps out into a clearing. Her hops grew longer. She was running now. Did she feel insecure in the open? Faster and faster she hopped and then . . . she vanished.

The end of her story was brutal: on each side of her last prints a snow angel registered lightly in powder. Feathers. A sweep of wings—the embrace of an owl. At the center a dot of cherry. The period at the end of the sentence.

•

I turned back then. What was the point of heading on? The snow was blinding now, the trace almost lost. The coyote kept going higher into the woods, and Lola's legs had accumulated heavy snow stockings. I had my kill already, and found out what I'd wanted before I'd begun: the coyotes were heading exactly where Lola had taken me all autumn: crossing eastward from the brook to Owl's Head. They weren't coming anywhere near the goats. I'd suspected as much since October. Now I had printed confirmation.

PART IV

Aging

Pastorals

Singing has always been associated with shepherds, for it wouldn't seem natural for . . . businessmen to indulge their passions in song.

—MOLIERE

IN HIS SEMINAL CLASSIC ON THE NUER OF SUDAN, THE anthropologist E. E. Evans-Pritchard writes: "The Nuer, like most pastoral peoples, are poetic and most men and women compose songs which are sung at dances and concerts or are composed for the creator's own pleasure and chanted by him in lonely pastures and amid the cattle in camp kraals."

The generalization is a bit startling—*Like most pastoral people the Nuer are poetic*—coming from such an esteemed anthropologist of the twentieth century. For Evans-Pritchard seems to assert that the majority of people who herd animals have a "poetic" frame of mind and their daily involvement with domestic ungulates somehow makes them burst into song.

The idea of the poetic herder—the singing cowboy, the flute-tooting shepherd boy—has always been a staple of pastoral mythology; and a quick survey of the world's pastoral people does, indeed, reveal an odd penchant for poetry and song: The Kalasha herdsmen of the Hindu Kush have special poems of praise—*ispadek*—for their favorite goats. Sami reindeer herders once sang *yoik* to their reindeer. Basque shepherds engage in *bertsolari* singing and poetry competitions both in Spain and North America, where they emigrated to work sheep in the West. Poetry is held in high regard among Somali camel herders, who have different songs for driving camels, loading camels, and bringing them back to the corral (poetry competitions are also a staple of Somali pastoral life). In the Andes, herding songs reach back all the way to the Incas, who developed their own pastoral poetry. Swedish cowherds, Armenian shepherds, Sicilian, Bulgarian, Indian herders—the list goes on of pastoral people who composed verse in the course of their work. So if Evans-Pritchard was right, what makes herders seemingly inclined to song?

Herders the world over "talk" to their animals in song. Sometimes they use flutes or horns, whistles or harps. Yet the instrument of choice—it's hard to lose or break—is the human voice. We quickly learned with our own goats that voice was a useful tool. I could calm a confused and screaming kid with the sound of my voice alone, even if she couldn't see me. A shrill falsetto could get a lagging doe to prick up her ears and come running to the rest of the herd. The goats understood the meaning of different tones and pitches, and since *they* were so vocal, we became vocal too; and we spent our days around the farmstead calling back and forth to each other from the house to the paddock. Dona developed a special singsong greeting, a call-and-response they got to know. It didn't necessarily "mean" anything other than "I'm here." If we wanted to call them in from the pasture we used a different call.

Wherever people milked cows or goats (sheep, mares, yaks,

or camels) they sang as well. Milking songs are found throughout the globe, from the Hebrides to sub-Saharan Africa to Mongolia. "Men and women have not been singing at the milking for the past thousand years or so merely to exercise their lungs," writes David Mackenzie in *Goat Husbandry*. "A consistent singer can make the milk drip from the goat's or cow's teats merely by singing the accustomed songs. For a goat distracted by a breach of routine, or a tender udder, the accustomed song or the regular patter of soothing nonsense is the best aid to let-down available."

One way herders got their animals' attention was through a high octave-leaping falsetto: the yodel. While we think of the yodel as uniquely Swiss, it exists in various forms throughout the world, from central Africa to the Solomon Islands. The biomusicologist Nils Wallin found that the high pitch range of yodeling has the strongest "recognition effect" on domestic cattle. Wallin believes that the yodel was an important tool in creating a "new relationship between man and animal" during the Neolithic. He posits that yodeling arose when humans shifted from hunting to herding and that it helped humans domesticate wild animals.

The women herders of Sweden had their own version of yodeling—*kulning*. Like the yodel, *kulning* consists of high nasal tones and simple melancholy melodies; it's the oldest form of music known in Scandinavia. Through *kulning,* the *valkulla* talked to their cows and goats throughout the day over miles of boreal forests, and could call them home at night. There's a haunting, magical quality to *kulning*. When I first heard a recording of *kulning* it raised the hair on my neck. I went outside and played the CD across the lawn. All the goats ran out of the barn and stood mesmerized, ears raised, and stayed that way throughout the whole recording.

From then on we incorporated our own version of *kulning* into our calls.

If the human voice proved such an effective tool to the herder, why not ornament it with song or verse? Or why not take the unconscious beauty of a herding song and turn it into a literary piece? Pastorals and bucolics were originally herding songs (*pastoralis* means "shepherd"; *boukolos,* "cow-herding song"). Professional poets, from antiquity onward, appropriated herders' songs and transformed them into literary art. Pastorals became songs sung *about* herders, not *by* them. Already by the Middle Ages, shepherds and goatherds became romanticized figures in poems written by people who had little sense of what it was actually like to herd sheep. Pastorals became a literary trope of the leisure class.

Literary pastorals first appeared in Mesopotamia, yet probably existed thousands of years earlier. The psalms of the shepherd-king David followed in the pastoral tradition—*The Lord is my shepherd; I shall not want. He maketh me to lie down in green pastures.* So did verses in later books of the Bible (Proverbs and Song of Solomon, among others). The Syracuse poet Theocritus wrote his *Idylls* about Sicilian shepherds and goatherds in the third century B.C. They became the model for Virgil, who reset the poems for a Roman audience three centuries later and named them *Eclogues.* More polished and self-conscious than Theocritus' rustic originals, Virgil's *Eclogues* employed the same characters and themes: unrequited love, an obsession with lactating animals, the challenging poem, the longing for a golden age. These subjects became the staples of literary pastorals that followed. In the Middle Ages, French troubadours composed *pastourelles.* In the Italian Renaissance, Dante and Petrarch wrote eclogues.

Pastoral narrative romances of the late Renaissance were, arguably, the first novels ever written (and the model for Cervantes' *Don Quixote*). In England, John Donne and Edmund Spenser wrote eclogues (Spenser called eclogues "Goteheard Tales," but the word means "little sketch"). The English Romantic poets Wordsworth, Keats, and Coleridge recapitulated the wandering work of the shepherd with their famous walking tours. The only things missing were the sheep.

One of the touchstones of literary pastorals is the "singing competition," or the "poetic challenge." Two or more herders gather at noon under a tree and exchange verses—and often insults—in a cutting competition, like "playing the dozens" or the Scottish flyting. The tradition lives on today in rap and hip-hop as well as in the Arabic *zajal*. But you find it alive also among Bedouin and Somali herders and a few decades ago among Greek and Sicilian herders. The social anthropologist Sandra Ott describes the poetic challenge as perfectly preserved among Basque shepherds in the Pyrenees as late as the1940s. *Xikito* was a form of ritual verbal dueling conducted by men on transhumance. Two shepherds stood apart on a mountainside and hurled rhymed four-line verses at each other. They did this, Ott explains, "until their anger was spent." One typical insult was to accuse your adversary in verse of having sex with a sow.

Poetry is often the making not of sense but *non*sense. Good poetry bypasses the head and enters the heart without the gray matter getting in the way. Poetry must resist logic, as Wallace Stevens said, "almost completely." The English words *chant* and *incant* and *enchant* all derive from the same word for "song." The gods gave Orpheus the gift of poetry and song expressly to *communicate with animals.* Animal talk doesn't have to make sense to make the milk come down. A "patter of soothing nonsense" will do. Poetry brings us back to a preverbal world we once shared with other animals, where our sense of sound was highly emotive and connotative. One of the few modes of speech that give us access to other animals, says the poet Gary Snyder, and produce "a deep sense of communion and communication with nature and with specific non-human beings . . . is poetry and song."

I didn't know when I started raising goats that such a profound and ancient connection existed between herding animals and song. I'd always unwittingly loved pastorals (from the epic of *Gilgamesh* to the poems of Robert Frost). They all shared a quixotic nostalgia for a world that once seemed more complete than ours: a dreamtime, a golden age, a Garden of Eden. This longing turns out not to be modern at all, but as old as the first written texts. *Gilgamesh* laments the age when Enkidu was one with the animals—before he became domesticated himself. Every pastoral since has been part elegy, a yearning for a time when humans weren't separated from the animal Other, but understood implicitly what each one "said." Every pastoral is the dream of a common language; and I've been searching for such a language all along. I've caught fleeting glimpses here and there on walks in the woods with my goats when we share a footprint, a rhythm, a key. When I sing to them and they sing back I think I know what they say—but the only way to tell it is in psalms.

In his ethnography on the Nuer of Sudan, E. E. Evans-Pritchard recorded a poem sung by a Nuer herder. She was not a professional or literary poet, but a young unlettered girl who'd come in from the fields after watching her cattle all day.

What's remarkable about her poem is that it contains all the elements of earlier and later literary pastorals: a lament, a challenge, a love song to her herds, and one eye gazing at God.

The wind blows my wind,
Where does it blow to?
It blows to the river
The shorthorn carries its full udder to the pastures
Let her be milked by my sister
Ever quarreling Rolnyang
My belly will be filled with milk.
This country is overrun by strangers
They throw our ornaments into the river
They draw their water from the bank
Black hair my sister
I am bewildered
Black hair my sister I am bewildered
We gaze at the stars of God

Pilgrimage

WE BRED THE GOATS AGAIN. FOUR OF THEM NOW CHAUFfeured to the buck one by one. The next spring Hannah threw a singlet: a caramel-colored buckling. Lizzie twin doelings again; Pie two spotted siblings—a brother and sister. Nisa birthed her babies in the woods one sunny afternoon beneath a tamarack tree, two midnight black twins with chocolate eye stripes, a buckling and a tiny doe—the last and most beautiful of the lot. The herd stood now at thirteen head.

That second year we had no difficulty milking. Hannah bonded briefly with her kid and surprised us all: she was easy to milk. So were the new mothers, Nisa and Pie. Lizzie, as always, was perfect. We never once lost a milk pail that year.

Over the previous winter we'd set up a milk room in the basement of the house. One side of the room let out to ground level and the rest lay under earth, so the room stayed cool all summer. The room already had plumbing and a cement floor—perfect for processing milk and making cheese. We salvaged an old double-basin, seven-foot stainless steel sink and installed it in the room. In one basin, I could set a ten- or fourteen-gallon pot to act as a cheese vat. The other basin would be for cleaning, the long drain board for molding and draining cheese. All we needed now was to find out what kind of cheese to make.

The art of cheesemaking may have sprung up simultaneously throughout many parts of the world, but in France the craft reached its fullest and most diverse expression. The culture, the different climates (dry Mediterranean to North Atlantic to Alpine), the natural caves throughout the south (perfect for aging cheese), and an ancient relationship with various breeds of ruminants all conspired in France to produce an encyclopedic amount of cheeses and methods of making them.

If I wanted to learn to make a hard aged cheese I needed to go to France. I needed to make a pilgrimage to a region specifically like our own—mountainous, with cold winters, wet springs, and short summers. A place where exquisite goat cheeses were made by hand on isolated mountain farms and done this way, continuously, for centuries. I needed to go, in short, to the Pyrenees.

In April I found a woman who lived in the department of Ariège in the central Pyrenees—the mountainous Couserans region. She was willing to introduce me to a few neighboring cheesemakers who lived on small farms and milked their own goats. Kim Chevalier had one request: Vermont maple syrup—the only thing she wanted from the United States. I was delighted to bring her some bottles, a taste of our own *terroir*. I'd pack them in my luggage double-sealed in ziplock bags.

I booked my flight in May. Dona would stay home and milk the goats. I left for France the second week of June.

•

The tiled floors of the Toulouse airport were sticky. I kept lifting up my shoe and wondering, *Who sprayed soda all over the floor?* I'd been in transit for thirty hours. Albany, New York, to Newark. Newark to Paris overnight. A five-hour layover at Charles de Gaulle. Then the flight south to Blagnac Airport.

At the Avis counter I chatted with two young women about the Pyrenees. I showed them pictures of my goats. Strange American man, they must have thought, carrying photographs of goats. Yet I was excited and hadn't slept and the drive down to the Pyrenees would take two hours.

At the airport café I stopped for tea. Why were the floors all over Blagnac Airport sticky? Everyone kept lifting their expensive Parisian heels and cursing. I grabbed my bag and the black nylon was drenched, tacky to the touch. *The maple syrup*!

Across the floor, a thin slick of amber betrayed my path. The Yankee boob with photos of goats was leaking *terroir* all over the arrival lounge.

At the men's room sink I found the offending bottle and a leaflet inside the sopped bag. The Transportation Security Administration's "Notice of Baggage Inspection." They'd opened one of the syrup bottles back in Newark and hadn't sealed it again. "Smart Security Saves Time," the leaflet read. American Homeland Security was making the world safe from *terroir*.

June was still cold in the Couserans. The rains had swelled the Salat River and columbine bloomed along the roads. The Ferme de Rouze sat in clouds at over three thousand feet. We'd switchbacked through the forest above Ustou and arrived at the farm in the rain. A cluster of stone barns pressed against a steep mountainside. It was Monday and we'd come for the morning cheesemaking. Alpine goats watched us from inside the barn, large brown does with beards and long back-curving horns. When the clouds lifted for a few seconds, the snow peaks loomed dramatically above.

On their mountaintop, Caroline and Jean-Pierre Gatti made beautiful raw-milk *tommes* from a herd of sixty Alpines and Saanens. Their farm sat along the GR 10, the hiking trail that follows the spine of the Pyrenees. Aside from making cheese, the Gattis ran a small hiking hostel—a *gîte d'étape*—for passing hikers where they served their own milk-fed pigs, kids, lamb, and charcuterie. And, of course, their cheese.

Caroline Gatti greeted us at the wooden door of the milk house. She had blue eyes and yellow hair pulled back in a tie. She wore a long white apron and white rubber boots and handed Kim and me a box of plastic booties to slip over our shoes. The barn lay to the left, the cheese rooms to the right. Caroline ushered us down an alley where panels of Plexiglas gave a view of either side. Her husband was just finishing the morning milking. Six does ate grain on a raised platform, electric milkers attached to udders. The last of their milk had just run through a pipe to the cheese room, where it filtered directly into a hundred-gallon vat. There it mingled with yesterday's milk and was ready to be made into cheese.

Caroline made cheese three times a week April through October—twelve *tommes* at a time, over two hundred pounds of cheese a month. She made fresh *crottin* once a week. All this she explained in the energetic French of her native Alsace-Lorraine as we walked through the milk house. She kept stopping now and then to see if I understood.

The cheese room was moist and steamy with sweet-smelling milk, the vat already filled and seeded with the starter. Caroline was waiting now to add the rennet, the *preseur*. The room was covered floor to ceiling with orange tiles, and the whey from the cheesemaking could be poured directly into a floor drain (where it went to a lower level of the barn to feed the pigs). Everything on the farm had to be immaculate; inspections are rigorous for organic and unpasteurized dairies. The Gattis couldn't simply cook uncleanliness away.

While we waited to add the rennet to the vat, Caroline showed us her cave, a paneled room down the hall kept at a steady 57 degrees Fahrenheit. *Tommes* sat on rough pine shelves; hundreds of them the size of birthday cakes in various stages of ripening. The younger wheels were white with a fuzz of bluish mold, the older ones the color of nectarines. The three- and four-month-old *tommes* had a hard orange rind. These were ready to be eaten or sold. A distributor would drive up the mountain to collect them the following day. He sold the Gattis' *tommes* all over France.

That rainy morning at the Ferme de Rouze we made *tommes*. Caroline walked me through all the stages: the renneting and hardening, the cutting of the curd with a harp, the cooking and stirring. She showed me how to mold and unmold *tommes* in their forms. She had no trade secrets, but shared everything—her times and temperatures and techniques. At one point while we were waiting for the curd to set, we went back to the cave and washed *tommes* with salt water and brushed the older wheels. I wasn't sure how it would've worked in reverse, had a Frenchman arrived at an American dairy with camera, paper, pen, and a ton of questions. Perhaps artisanal cheesemakers are the same around the world, as no two cheeses could ever possibly be the same, so reliant are they on the particulars of place. Or perhaps the mark of the artisan is that he or she gives away their craft, that culture is passed in this way, without trademarks or copyrights—but as a simple gift. For it was a gift standing in Caroline Gatti's tiled cheese room that morning learning every aspect of her craft.

In her kitchen during a break, when we finally got off our feet, our conversation turned—of course—to goats. Caroline's face grew more animated than before. We talked of feed and hoofs and horns. Milk stones, bucks, breeding, and herd queens. We were like ham radio operators who'd discovered a similar passion, and chattered on while Kim listened and sometimes translated. You need humility, Caroline expounded, to live with goats—and you need a good sense of humor. Goats, she said, are the same size and weight as us. They can stand on two feet at our height, and even their eyes remind us of a version of ourselves; and if they like you they'll lick your face, and if they don't—watch out. As for sheep—which she and her husband also raised—she had little to say on the subject, only that a leg of lamb tasted awfully good.

I spent twelve days in the Pyrenees. I tried a lot of cheese. The bloomy-rind *crottins,* the tangy Bethmale, the golden Moulis cow cheese, *brebis* from Massat. I visited other cheesemakers on mountain farms. I thought I'd try cheese from all over the country, but since nearly every valley in the Ariège had its own cheesemaker, it seemed pointless to eat cheese from farther away. I kept my tasting local.

At that time of year in the Pyrenees the sheep and cows and horses were heading up to the mountains to their summer pastures—the *estives*—the transhumance under way. One morning I hiked with six hundred Tarrascon sheep up to the mountains. A pair of Great Pyrenees herding dogs—*le patou*—led the way, scouting and marking the mountain road ahead of the herd. Next came three shepherds with black berets and herding sticks; a river of sheep trotted right behind at a furious pace, six abreast, canvas-colored, and noisy; they sounded like a baritone men's choir, painfully out of tune. Behind the sheep, a border collie wove in and out of legs, snapping at any slow ones and racing up trailside cliffs to collect the laggards. I marched behind with dozens of locals and tourists. We made a human wall to keep driving the sheep along the narrowing trail.

All morning we walked beside the icy Lez River up into the Biros Valley. Water dripped from rocks along the way. Mount Crabère stood with its glaciers at the head of the valley. The day turned glorious with sun and alpine flowers; and I found myself moved nearly to tears inside that flood of sheep, among that ancient pageant of animals and people hiking side-by-side—a real transhumance, that which I mimicked in miniature back home in Vermont. In that part of the Pyrenees they no longer milked their ewes or cows on the *estives* during summer transhumance. The sheep I walked among that day were all, alas, destined to be meat.

At the Ferme de Rouze we finished making cheese in the early afternoon. Before I left Caroline Gatti's kitchen, she put a hand on my wrist and said wait, and flew upstairs. The rain had stopped outside, and a bit of blue hung in the cold mountain air. Kim Chevalier and I waited by the screen door. Caroline came down the steps with a printout from her computer. "Protocole de Fabrication Tomme," it read. Typed on the sheet were the exact times and temperatures for making her *tomme*. I thanked her profusely. She knew she was handing me something precious. A recipe. A gift.

•

Culture is the starter that goes into a cheese but it's also the starter for all our human leavening. It's passed from one person to another and on to the next generation. When I drove back down the Gattis' mountain that afternoon, I knew at last what kind of cheese I'd make back in Vermont. A *tomme* just like Caroline Gatti's *tommes de Rouze*. A cheese made from goats and clouds, humility and mountain air.

Affinage

Every time you begin a good work, you must pray to him most earnestly to bring it to perfection.

—THE RULE OF ST. BENEDICT

SUMMER CAME AGAIN IN VERMONT. WE WERE MILKING four goats now, the herd in their July glory—shiny coats, full udders. Lizzie was fully recovered in her burnt orange mantle, Hannah in her golden raiment; seven kids leaped across the lawn. We found homes for all the kids that year, even the bucklings. They'd be castrated and turned into wethers.

In the evenings I made Caroline Gatti's *tomme*. We'd gutted an old pie safe, screened its front and sides, and set it in the root cellar of the house. The screened cabinet had room for about fifteen wheels of cheese. The conditions in the cellar seemed almost perfect for aging a *tomme,* 59 degrees and 90 percent humidity most days. The walls were stone, the floor earth. We had no idea if the right microorganisms would thrive there or the *tommes* turn out okay. There was nothing to do but make the cheese and see.

•

The life history of a cheese is not unlike that of a person. A good cheese gathers virtue as it ages. It develops depth and character. Cheesemakers sometimes speak of the stages a cheese goes through on its way to maturity as a "journey." The cheese arrives at certain landmarks along the way: the milestones of pH or acidity; the way station of one type of mold or another developing on its skin; the achievement of a certain texture and consistency—the pâte—inside its body. The art of aging cheese is called *affinage,* which means in French "refining" or "making finer." To become refined a cheese needs the correct environment. It needs patience and vigilance. The cheesemaker needs yet another thing: faith. The faith part was new to me. There are no recipes for that. Fortunately there are for making cheese.

Cheese is the slowest of all slow foods. If you want to get there fast, eat American. Each recipe is a journey, a meander toward perfection.

1. *Chauffage*—heating, warming

Day One. 7:00 p.m.

Sunday, the last week of July. I've come in from the evening milking with three gallons of warm goat milk sloshing in a stainless steel milk can. I'm making a *tomme* this evening. The windows are thrown wide and outside a catbird jazzes in a lilac bush. I pour the milk into a ten-gallon vat; and this is how a cheese begins its life: as milk straight from the animal's udder. Without the freshest unpasteurized milk I can't attempt a perfect cheese. No matter how excellent my culture, my cave, my cutting and molding of curds—without the highest-quality milk from an animal eating grass my cheese will show its imperfections with age.

I've got ten gallons of milk tonight from four milkings. The oldest milk is from yesterday morning (only thirty-four hours old). Artisanal cheesemakers use milk no older than forty hours. The fresher the better. Milk from only one milking is best.

My "vat" is a ten-gallon stainless steel pot that sits snugly inside a sink basin filled with water. The hot water bath will gently raise the temperature of the milk. I drop a floating thermometer inside the vat, and after a minute it reads 78 degrees. I've got to wait for the milk's temperature to rise another ten degrees, then I can start to make cheese.

Cheesemakers call the place they make cheese the "make room." My basement make room has a sink, a fridge, a stainless steel table, an icebox for cooling milk, and a few open shelves for drying and storing milk pails, cans, and buckets. Best of all, there's a large ground-floor window with a view of the mountain across the valley. From here in the evening I can watch the color of the mountain change as the sun sets on its flanks—apricot to burnt sienna to brown. The shade creeps up the slope like a curtain rolling up the day. The mountain soars nearly three thousand feet above the valley floor. The Mohawk people who once lived here called the mountain "The Top" or "The Place at the Very Top." Today a monastery sits up there protected by hundreds of acres of forest. The Charterhouse of the Transfiguration is the only Carthusian monastery in North America and closed to all visitors. Sometimes in spring when the Northern Spys blossom down here, snow paints the mountaintop. It's a lovely sight, the pink apple blossoms, white snow, lime green leaves, but the color scheme never lasts long.

2. *Ensemencement*—sowing, seeding

7:43 p.m.

The thermometer in the vat reads 88 degrees now—I've been checking all this time. The last throw of light lies across the mountain, a body in recline. Down here I can't see the mountaintop or the monastery but know at this hour the monks have eaten and prayed. Even though the day still burns up there the brothers are probably all in bed.

The milk looks porcelain white in my vat, with a darker meniscus of butterfat floating on its surface. The milk is warm enough now to receive its starter culture, to be "seeded." I scoop a quarter teaspoon of a freeze-dried culture from a foil bag. I'm using a different starter culture than the one I use for chèvre. This one's an MM 100 lactic starter, which contains different bacteria isolated in a lab from some of the best hard cheeses in France—*Lactococcus lactis* subsp. *lactis, L. lactis* subsp. *cremoris, L. lactis* subsp. *lactis* biovar. *diacetylactis*. The culture consists of large yellow flakes that smell a bit like brewer's yeast. It's the same culture Caroline Gatti uses in France.

I agitate the milk up and down with a long white plastic paddle; and when the milk turns over top to bottom, I sprinkle flakes into the liquid. I row roughly, lift the paddle, and replace the lid on the vat. Now I must wait for the starter culture to inoculate the milk, the bacteria to multiply and "ripen," and acid formation begin. This will take about forty-five minutes. There's nothing to do but loiter and let the microbes do their work.

English has no sufficient translation for the word *tomme*. The word in French means "volume" or "tome" as in a "book," yet can also signify "a wheel of cheese." *Tommes* are ancient mountain cheeses made historically from goat milk on small farms where the milk supply was limited. I like that my cheese is called a tome, because making a cheese is somewhat like making a book. Both take raw material from the world and transfigure it into art. Both are the products of rumination—animal and human. When you make a cheese you do a little work with the milk then wait and come back later and do some more, and wait again. It takes months to make a cheese. A book takes even longer. You can't make either in one go. Time is the essential element. Time cures the imperfections, one hopes, in both.

The *tomme* I'm making today will age inside a cellar for several months; its character will keep changing from day to day, and week to week. At four months the *tomme* will have a wonderfully complex and savory taste, its body cream-colored and firm with small eyelets no larger than sesame seeds. Unlike my body, my *tomme* will grow firmer, not flabbier, with age. Time removes the excess moisture in a cheese and pares it down. But you never know how a *tomme* or a book will turn out. This is where the faith comes in.

3. *Emprésurage*—forwarding, making eager: adding rennet

8:35 p.m.

An hour has fled. I closed the kids in for the night then stood outside and watched a heron fly across the pond. A streak of fire hung in the dusk over Bennetts Ridge.

Back in the make room the milk smells yeasty and sweet. The starter culture has gone to work. If I were a commercial cheesemaker I'd be taking a pH reading at this point to check the acidity of the milk. I'd keep charting the pH level (or the titratable acid level) throughout the cheesemaking process to make sure the developing curds were following a strict "schedule of acidification." Since I'm new to this and my *tommes* don't have to turn out the same each time, I do it the old-fashioned way—by observation and feel. Some of the guesswork and mystery would disappear if I used a pH meter; and one day it may come to that.

I grab a plastic bottle of rennet from the fridge and with a syringe pull up 3.9 cc of brown liquid. I've got to add just the right amount of rennet. If I use too much the cheese will turn rubbery or "corky" as it ages. Too little and I'll lose a lot of curd, or the cheese might not even firm up properly. Since the fats and proteins and minerals in the milk change from day to day, the amount of rennet I use does too. I'm still figuring the amount for each *tomme* I make. The knowledge comes with years of knowing your herd's lactation and how it changes with the weather and season. It may take a lifetime to learn. I do the best I can. 3.9 cc of rennet for now seems to work.

I paddle the milk in the vat again. The liquid peaks and crests and I plunge the syringe and rennet squirts into the center. I oar the milk roughly from side to side and up and down until it sloshes, give it one more turn, then lift the paddle and let it drip. The milk whirlpools clockwise—a miniature ocean current. When the vat subsides into an equatorial calm, I replace the lid and check the clock. It's time to wait some more.

Cheese may not have been invented by monks and nuns, but without Catholic monasticism the variety and quality of cheese would be a lot poorer today. During the Middle Ages, while Europe fell to plague and war, monasteries became citadels of learning and retreat for the religious and those who opposed war. Built in out-of-the-way places, often on mountaintops, monasteries produced (among other things) books and cheese. Tomes and *tommes*. Monasteries tended to be self-reliant, and nuns and monks grew their own food. Because most monastic orders forbade eating meat, monasteries excelled at making a protein-rich alternative to flesh, namely cheese.

The number and variety of cheeses invented by nuns and

monks is impressive. Some of the best known include Munster, Port Salut, Bleu de Gex, Saint-Nectaire. Montasio, Pont l'Évêque, Bel Paese (some even argue mozzarella). In most cases the cheese simply took the name of its originating abbey. Munster cheese, for example, comes from the Vosges Mountains of Alsace and is itself a contraction of the word *monastery* in Latin (*monasterium*). Port Salut was originally named after the Trappist abbey of Notre-Dame de Port-du-Salut in Brittany. Abbeys gained reputations for the qualities of their cheese and established strict production controls (that form the basis of some of today's *appellation contrôlée* laws). Hard cheeses with their concentrated nutrition and portability were an ideal food, not just for monks and pilgrims on a journey but for laypeople too.

The Carthusian monks who live on top of our mountain don't make cheese. Neither do they make chartreuse—as the Carthusians do in France.

The only thing our monks produce is silence.

4. *Caillage*—curdling, congealing

8:38 p.m.

I've been paying close attention to the clock. So much of cheesemaking concerns time. How much comes and goes and how hours act on a body. Time transfigures one substance into another—I've been waiting for that all along.

My task now is to determine the minutes it takes for the milk in the vat to curdle, to reach what's called the "flocculation point." Knowing the precise flocculation point—from the time I added rennet—will tell how long I'll let the curds mature before cutting them. The flocculation point—the *caillage*—changes each time I make a cheese because the milk (and the weather) changes with each make. Yet there's a trick

I learned from the cheesemaker Peter Dixon, who learned it from a cheesemaker in France. I float a round flat plastic lid on the surface of the milk. As I wait for the milk to curdle I occasionally spin the lid. Immediately after adding the rennet the lid spins with no resistance. But as the caseins in the milk knit together into a tight weave the lid spins more slowly against the resistance of the stiffening curd. Eventually the lid will spin only half a turn, then a quarter turn, then not at all. The moment the milk reaches its flocculation point is when the lid spins a quarter turn.

I've been reaching down into the vat and spinning the plastic lid every few seconds. It moves fast at first, like a frictionless wheel of fortune. I'll have to wait several more minutes—I can tell by the speed of the spin. Twelve more minutes at least.

Of all the Catholic monastic orders the Carthusians are considered the most austere. The brothers on our mountain live alone in concrete cells, their hours spent in solitude and silence save for daily services in church and a weekly walk when they break their collective silence. Through extreme solitude, contemplation, and silence the monks are supposed to be drawn closer to God. They have no one else to talk to.

"Carthusians mark time not by decades, years, or days," explains the writer Nancy Klein. "Their time is out of time, directed . . . by the tolling of the immense church bell . . . in measured instants of the Latin 'now': *nunc, nunc, nunc*. For the monk, there is no future and no past, merely a series of 'nows.'"

5. *Durcissement*—hardening, stiffening

8:52 p.m.

Night increases outside. Venus swirls into view. The clock taps in the make room. I'm leaning over this low sink as if in prayer. I've been spinning and spinning the lid on the curd. Round and round it goes (*when it stops no one knows*). I'm stooping and spinning and night is advancing and I can hear it happen outside—crickets and bullfrogs, a barred owl—the night rounding itself from the west. And finally the lid spins only a half turn. Then a quarter: suddenly the milk has curdled. It's reached its flocculation point.

I stand and stretch. My knees crack. My neck aches. I consult the clock, do quick math, then write it out. I must wait now exactly forty-eight minutes for the curds to mature or "harden." Forty-eight minutes to let time and acidity do their labor. I replace the lid on the vat, remove my apron, and step outdoors. It's good to stand under the stars. The moon is a pewter harrow carving a path to the west.

Cheesemaking is contemplative work. It's work done usually in silence and often alone. It's no coincidence that monks and nuns excelled at such labor. In the sixth century a man named Benedict, the son of a Roman nobleman, founded a series of monasteries in a mountain valley eighty miles from Rome. Little is known about the life of Saint Benedict. He retreated to a cave in the mountains as a teenager, and lived there for three years, rejecting what he'd seen in the eternal city. His Rule of St. Benedict still serves as a rough guide for most Catholic monastic orders today. The rule stresses restraint of speech and food (no meat), common ownership of property, humility, and work. Since labor was viewed as a path to God, the rule specified the precise times of work: *from prime to the fourth hour in the morning* (6:00 to 10:00 a.m.) and *midway through the eighth hour, and then until Vespers* (2:30 to 6:00 p.m.). The remaining hours were passed in prayer, study, rest, and church.

Cheesemaking, with its strict schedule, proved particularly

suited to monastic life. Monasteries kept large flocks and thus had a plentiful supply of fresh milk. Saint Benedict wrote in his rule: "When they live by the labor of their hands, as our fathers and the apostles did, then they are really monks."

Down here in the valley I think often of the Carthusian brothers up on our mountain—especially when I make cheese. We live so close to each other, only altitude separates us, but their lives remain a mystery, a rumor, the sound of bells in the late afternoon. Still, I wonder what a day is like up there versus down here. The raven who's been rowing between our houses for weeks—a thin black line—do they see him too? The owl hooting now at night—do they hear his inflection? Do we share the same faith if not belief—the same lasting silence?

6. *Decaillage*—uncurdling, cutting the curd

9:40 p.m.

I tie on the apron again and remove the lid from the vat. The curd glistens inside, a glossy, seamless pool. It looks like yogurt—rich, yeasty, stiff—with a thin glaze of whey on top. The floating thermometer lies beached on a shoal of curds.

I check now for a "clean break" more out of formality than need (I can tell by the look that the curds have set up right). But I like the ritual of the clean break. I bury four fingers beneath warm curds, palm facing the ceiling. I nudge my middle finger up and the curd cracks in a straight tectonic line. The curds are ready to cut.

The curds for my *tomme* should be sliced roughly to the size of a corn kernel—"*grosseur des grains, blé à maïs,*" reads Caroline Gatti's recipe. And this is where the fun begins. Cheesemakers use long-handled metal harps to cut the curd in their cheese vats. The harps look like homemade instruments strung with four or five vertical strings (in Italy they're called "lyres"—the instruments traditionally carried by poets). Since my vat is so small, I use a long dull knife instead of a harp. I cut the virgin curds from side to side, then up and down. I make a tic-tac-toe board deep into the vat. I slash and flick and carve at forty-five-degree angles and work the curd at the bottom and the sides. I cut faster and faster until the cubes carve smaller and smaller and sink into the cloudy whey. I've stopped thinking of this substance now as milk; already it's transformed into something else—not quite cheese, but a material on its way to transfiguration. I've got to be patient now. We're getting closer to cheese all the time.

In a few minutes the curds are kernel size and sink like grain to the bottom of the vat, expressing more whey as they fall. I replace the floating thermometer inside and leave the curds to settle and heal for a few minutes. I step outside to moonlight for a breath.

From the age of twenty I carried around Thomas Merton's *Seven Storey Mountain* without ever actually reading it. In all the houses where I lived, Merton's book somehow came along. I must have known a day would come when I'd be ready to read the Trappist monk's autobiography about his religious conversion and entrance into monastic life. I liked what little I'd known of Merton but each time I opened *The Seven Storey Mountain* the text threw me out.

A book is like a key that fits into the tumbler of the soul. The two parts have to match in order for each to unlock. Then—*click*—a world opens.

The Seven Storey Mountain was published right after World War II and became an overnight bestseller, much to the surprise of both Merton and his publisher. In a world tired of war, the message of retreat and contemplation must have held fresh appeal. The mountain in the title refers to Dante's Mount Purgatory and the seven "storeys" or levels that encircle its slopes. Each level applies to one of the seven deadly sins. The conceit of Merton's autobiography lies in Dante's own theological notion that a soul can climb Mount Purgatory and slowly, with each terrace, perfect itself by shedding one sin after another. With all seven sins (or "taints") gone, the soul is refined and purified. At the summit of Purgatory, one finally reaches perfection. Union with God. One reaches Paradise.

Merton doesn't dwell on the metaphor of climbing Purgatory in his book. The soul perfecting itself is implicit in the text. He does say this: "I was not aware of the climbing I was about to have to do. The essential thing was to begin the climb."

7. *Brassage*—brewing, mixing, cooking

9:50 p.m.

The night is turning over. The sky increases with stars. The moon nests on Bennetts Ridge—it looks nothing like a wedge of cheese. I step back into the moist warmth of the make room. The lights are slightly blinding. Night seems to cling like liquid; I can't quite shake it off. The time has arrived to cook the curds. I must return to here and now . . . *Nunc. Nunc. Nunc.*

I scrub my hands and fingers. I scrub forearms and wrists and towel dry. Because the sink is low, I find the best way to slowly stir and break the curds is once again to kneel. This time on a low bench—a prie-dieu—while I attend the curds.

I drain the sink of its tepid water and turn the tap on hot. I want to raise the temperature in the vat slowly, one degree every two minutes. To assure a languid rise in heat, I keep throwing small increments of hot water into the sink—not too much at a time. Most cheesemakers use a vat lined with a hot-water jacket, which serves the same purpose.

Now I plunge the paddle into the vat and start to stir. I turn the curds with the paddle and feel them with the other hand. While I stir, I feel under the liquid for clumped-up curds and break them apart between fingers. Every once in a while I twist the hot tap and let a little heat into the sink. I check the thermometer often. I'm only at 90 degrees. I've got to reach 102 in forty minutes.

The concrete cells in which the Carthusians live on our mountain are meant to remind them of the caves in which both Saint Benedict and the Desert Fathers dwelled. Where and when the tradition of holy men living in caves began is hard to know, but Buddhist monks and Hindu *saddhus* retreated to caves long before Christ ever did. Perhaps the Christian tradition started with John the Baptist, who's said to have lived and baptized inside a cave. Saint Paul dwelled in a cave, as did Saint Francis, Saint Anthony, Saint Benedict, and Saint Ignatius Loyola (just to name a few). Why did all the saints live in caves? Was it that caves came rent-free and isolated and free from all the distractions of the world? Or that the saints could transform their souls in the dampness and silence under earth?

The monks on our mountain live a much more comfortable, though no less isolated, life than some of the earliest Christian hermits. Their cells are not under earth but in rooms with windows and a woodstove and a woodpile they keep meticulously stacked. Their cells *are* their cave, the place to make their souls ever finer. The Carthusian Rule states: "The monk, who continues faithfully in his cell and lets himself be molded by it, will gradually find that his whole life tends to become one continual prayer."

•

Twenty minutes have passed and I'm kneeling on this bench in a basement stirring a vat of curds—one hand in the liquid, the other on the paddle. The lamp throws shadows against the ceiling and the windows perspire steam; and this is my favorite part, when the whey turns warm and curds float in circles around my wrist and night presses in from outside; and here, kneeling over this warm, sweet cauldron I stir and weave a white substance while the motion and moist heat almost lull me to sleep. It feels a bit like "one continuous prayer."

Now the thermometer reads 101. The curds feel right to the touch. I squeeze a fistful and they bunch together nicely but break apart individually when I release them. I bounce the curds in an open palm, smell them, squeeze them. I shepherd them around the vat. They are doing exactly what they should. At 102 the cooking is done. I stop stirring; I stand and stretch. The curds sink swiftly to the bottom of the vat and disappear beneath the cloudy whey. I'll wait five minutes more for them to fully express themselves.

8. *Moulage*—molding, casting

10:30 p.m.

They made cheese at the Trappist monastery in rural Kentucky where Thomas Merton lived. Merton himself was not a cheesemaker—he wrote books. The monastery's abbot encouraged his bookmaking, and Merton wrote more than two dozen volumes of poetry, journals, and books of contemplation. While some monks at the Abbey of Gethsemani made volumes with milk, Merton filled his with verse. He didn't believe his particular craft was better than the other; they were both in the service of God.

•

The time has come to scoop the curds from my vat. The French word for cheese, *fromage,* comes from the Latin for "form" or "mold": a vessel in which a cheese is formed. The forms for my *tommes* are round and plastic and six inches high, their walls perforated with pea-size holes. I set two forms on the drain board then drape squares of unbleached muslin inside each.

Eighty percent of what's in the vat now is liquid whey. The curds have settled like pebbles to the bottom. I start by bailing whey off the top by using a saucepan. I dip the pan in the whey and empty it into a bucket to save for the neighbor's pigs. Pan after pan, the whey slowly wicks away and the vat empties and the curds on the bottom are revealed. When I've bailed off all I can, I pick up whole chunks of curd—they're already sticking together—and place them gently in the forms. Then I scoop up the rest of the curds with a colander and portion them in each form. I press the tepid curds with a flat palm and squeeze out whey to make room for yet more curds. One form is already filled to the top, and now the second is almost full. I top each form with the last balls of curd, then fold the muslin over the top of one, fit a plastic follower inside the form, and lean on the follower with both hands and all my weight. From each small hole in the form, whey shoots out in long streams like water from a dozen toy pistols.

Several abbeys in France have enormous cellars in which they age and store their cheese. The cheese cave at the Abbey of Tamié in Savoie lies directly under its cathedral, so inside the cave the workers (and the cheeses) can hear the choir singing; the cheeses are said to improve with all that song. The underground ripening rooms in such abbeys resemble library stacks, with rows and rows of shelves. Instead of books, they hold wheel after wheel of cheese. When aged properly, the cheeses turn into hardbacks.

9. *Retournement* (first)—turning, reversal

10:35 p.m.

I'm still pressing on the plastic follower with all my weight. The curds keeps squirting liquid like a garden sprinkler. In France they say a cheese "dries," not ages, because so much of *affinage* is about losing moisture, stripping away the inessential, the superfluous, paring down the body to its core.

I push down on the follower and with each squeeze the squirts grow thinner and thinner. One last push, then I pull up the follower, turn the form, shake the new *tomme* from its mold. It makes a small *thwuck* as it slips out. I strip the cloth from the *tomme*. The cheese is naked and white, five inches high. I drape the damp cloth back over the top of the form, turn the *tomme,* and place it back inside the opposite way. It slips into the form, taking the muslin with it. I wrap the top and replace the follower again and push. This time I balance a large rock on the follower and leave it there. I do the same with the second wheel. The rocks are green schist and round, both about ten pounds. We pulled them from the brook when the water was low.

The interiors of large cathedrals—Notre-Dame, St. Pauls, St. John the Divine—resemble enormous caves and caverns. The dark naves and apses and candlelit chapels are like grottoes under earth. Cathedrals, said Thomas Merton, are "caves of silence." Stony, quiet, echoey, slightly chilled. In a city they are islands of peace, silent places where you can be alone and anonymous and exist for a brief moment out of time. They remind me too of the prehistoric caves of southern Europe (Lascaux or Niaux or Trois Frères) where the most ancient human mysteries once took place. Like cathedrals, Paleolithic caves were places of transformation, liminal spaces between life and death, heaven and earth. "Mythogenetic zones," Joseph Campbell called them and said that *all* cathedrals and temples (in both east and west) derive from these original sacred caves. They represent the human race's first "manifestations of the magical space of God."

10. *Retournement* (second)—turning, reversal

10:49 p.m.

The two *tommes* sit now on the drain board encased in forms. Round stones perch on top of each. A thin cloudy rill of whey runs from the bottom of both into the sink. I haul the bucket of whey into the night, take a brief measure of the stars, breathe a bit of air, and duck back into the murky warmth of the make room. Now I've got to clean up all the mess. The vat, the colander, the utensils, the sink, the spoons, the thermometer, all the surfaces and the floor. In the middle of this I break to turn the *tommes* again. I take the rocks off the forms, unmold and undress, rewrap and press again. This is the second turning of the cheeses.

A new cheese dies in a sense and is wrapped in a shroud, salted or hung up to dry, then put inside a cave where it refines itself—covered in the aspect of death (with molds and smears and yeast). After a number of days the cheese is purified and reborn, removed from the cave and shared with the world. The cheese is transformed. The cheese is transfigured. Inside it's angelic white and feeds the body and the soul. A wafer to be shared with the world.

Does this story sound familiar?

The more I made cheese the more uncanny the parallels I saw between its making and the Passion of Christ. Here's just a few:

> There are fourteen stations of the cross, and fourteen stages of making an aged cheese.
>
> Veronica wiped the salt from Jesus' face with a cotton cloth. A cheesemaker wipes the face of a cheese with a cotton cloth dipped in salt water.
>
> Jesus fell three times on the way to his crucifixion. A cheese is turned three times on its way to drying.
>
> Jesus was stripped of his clothes before being hung on the cross. A cheese is stripped of its cloth before being hung—or shelved—to dry.
>
> Mary Magdalene washed Jesus' feet. In France cheese is called "the feet of the Gods."
>
> Cheese, remarked Clifton Fadiman, is milk's "leap toward eternity." Jesus *is* eternal.
>
> In Wisconsin I once saw a bumper sticker that read: *I believe in Cheeses*!

All cheesy puns aside, it *is* curious that cheese was developed most ardently in Christian cultures and wasn't made historically in non-Judeo-Christian lands, like India, East Asia, or the indigenous Americas and Australia. Did the story of Christ's Passion suggest itself as a metaphor—and a recipe—for early Christian cheesemakers? Or did the natural history of a cheese inform the story of Christ's transfiguration, his passion and resurrection? Does the magic of making cheese somehow suggest the supernatural or a miracle?

On the drain board the cheeses weep—drop by drop by drop.

11. *Retournement* (third)—turning, reversal

11:00 p.m.

How is a soul like a cheese? It starts out raw and unformed and tries to refine itself over time. It is constantly corrected and rebuffed, purged of blemishes and taints and sins.

In some American Catholic schools, nuns once showed their students photographs of a glass of milk and told them: *This is what your soul looks like*. They urged the boys and girls to keep their souls as pure as milk. If milk is a metaphor for the soul in its pure state, what then is cheese but the soul refined to perfection?

I turn the *tommes* over the last time and replace the rocks on top. They'll stay this way through the night, expressing whey. I hang the pots and colander and put the utensils in place. Any second now on the mountaintop the monastery bells will ring. The monks will wake in the cells. Their "night office" will begin, the Little Hours for Our Lady in their cells. Even in the middle of the night the Carthusian brothers wake to prayer.

12. *Démoulage*—unmolding

Day Two. 6:35 a.m.

We've all passed the night in silence. The humans upstairs. The cheeses downstairs. The monks on the mountain. The goats in the barn. The sun fans weakly through the window. I've woken late this morning and come down here first thing to see how my *tommes* fared the night. Everything looks right.

No more whey seeps from the forms. The rocks remain in place. If there'd been something wrong with the curds, if they'd harbored harmful bacteria, the cheeses would've bloated by now and cast the rocks off their followers. But they're sitting on the drain board in the morning light looking quite fit. The smell is good too. Slightly yeasty—like bread dough.

I remove the rocks first, then the followers, and turn the forms upside down. It takes a few seconds for the *tommes* to drop from their molds. I strip them of their muslin. They are chalk white and firm and round, their faces impressed with each crease of the cloth. I set them side by side on squares of rough-hewn spruce. They look lovely sitting in morning sun, waiting to enter the cave. When Sicilian cheesemakers remove the curds from their vat, swaddled in cloth, they call the new cheese "*bambinos*." Caroline Gatti called her new cheeses her "babies." These are my *bambinos* today. Two white cheeses sitting in morning sun.

Books, too, become finer with time; with hours and months and years they lose their inessentials and purify themselves. Thomas Merton's own books became more nuanced and refined as his own soul aged. *The Seven Storey Mountain* has a brittle, autohortatory tone at times, as if he were trying to spur himself on with his new convictions. The older he grew, the more comfortable he became with his faith and—most notably—*other* faiths.

Merton began to see parallels between all monasticisms. He grew intrigued by Zen and Buddhism. At fifty-three he traveled to Asia to meet, among others, the Dalai Lama. Despite his months of rural retreat in Kentucky, he was by then the most famous monk in America. Widely photographed and quoted, outspoken against the Vietnam War, Merton was so excited by his trip to Asia that he wrote in his journal upon leaving: "The moment of take-off was ecstatic. The window wept jagged shining courses of tears. Joy. We left the ground—I with Christian mantras and a great sense of destiny, of being at last on my true way after years of waiting and wondering and fooling around. May I not come back without having settled the great affair."

What was "the great affair"? Some say he wanted to go off into the Himalayas and study with a Buddhist master. No one really knows, though it's clear his Catholic faith hadn't changed—only deepened. Before he was due to give a lecture in Bangkok one afternoon, he stepped out of his hotel's bathtub and touched a fan with faulty wiring—and was electrocuted on the spot. Many saw self-prophecy in the last lines of *The Seven Storey Mountain,* penned decades earlier:

> Do not ask when it will be or where it will be or how it will be: On a mountain or in a prison, in a desert or in a concentration camp or in a hospital or at Gethsemani . . . You will not know until you are in it. But you shall taste the true solitude of my anguish and my poverty and I shall lead you into the high places of my joy and you shall die in Me and find all things in my mercy which has created you for this end . . . That you may become the brother of God and learn to know the Christ of the burnt men.

13. *Salage*—salting

6:45 a.m.

I've been standing here admiring my two *tommes*. How they'll age I cannot say. So much depends upon the time to come, about what happens in the air, the atmosphere. The weather. About time itself. The mystery of minutes and hours.

I've taken out a sack of Sel de Guérande. The sea salt is gray and coarse and looks like road salt. I scoop a generous handful from the bag and smother the face of one cheese. Take another handful and smooth it over the next. The salt will pull water from the cheese and make it weep. It will protect it from unwanted bacteria and add flavor to the *tomme.* Tomorrow morning I'll scrape the undissolved salt off the first face, turn the *tommes,* and spread more salt on the other side.

Topped with gray salt the *tommes* look like wedding cakes sprinkled with roadside gravel.

Even before I lived in the shadow of a monastery—before I ever dreamed of making cheese—monks fascinated me. The notion of retreat was immensely appealing, of tucking myself away from the world and growing my own food. I grew up in a house beside a thundering parkway in the suburbs of New York City and the sound of traffic in the morning and the radio blaring 1010 WINS was to me an echo of despair. The world of shopping malls and suited men on commuter trains reading *The New York Times* was a waiting cage I longed to escape before I'd entered. A monastic life may have seemed like a wonderful alternative—a contemplative life of rural retreat and self-reliance on top of a mountain. The problem was, I knew no monks nor monasteries, and I also happened to be a Jew.

At nineteen I quit college, saved money, and traveled to India for a year. For months I lived in the basement of a monastery in the foothills of the Himalayas. This was in Dharamsala and the monks were Tibetan Buddhists, and the Dalai Lama lived just down the road. I woke each morning to the sound of bells and cymbals, the monks chanting *puja* and doing their *jukai* singing. Outside the basement window spread a dazzling view of snow peaks. There were goatherds in the woods, waterfalls where I washed my clothes. The monks were young and friendly and tried to teach me to sing in overtones. I liked being in the basement, a secular among the brothers, hearing the lovely chanting. Nothing was required of me. Time seemed to stand still. I was supremely happy for a while. I tried meditation and took classes—but I was never very serious. I decided eventually I wasn't ready for that kind of life. I needed to finish college. I also wanted to make books.

And now I find myself a world away in a basement too, with a window letting out on to mountains and the bells of a monastery nearby and the monks—if I could hear them—chanting their morning prayers. We make a circle of our life and never know it. We hardly pay time its due. The bells here are little different from those in Dharamsala, or the bells that hang from the necks of my goats. Each is a call to prayer, the tongue of the bell saying *nunc, nunc, nunc.* Does it matter the bell one chooses?

14. *Affinage*—maturing, ripening; becoming finer

6:50 a.m.

It can take as little as two months for a cheese to perfect itself but a soul takes so much longer. How does a soul perfect itself? By turning itself over and over so often it forgets whose house it lives in—and whose form. By losing piece by piece what it loves best: its self.

Catholics have only one lifetime to reach perfection but Hindus and Buddhists say a soul takes many lifetimes—and reincarnations—before it can reach *moksha,* or transcendence. At that point the soul is released from the cycle of birth and death and doesn't have to be reborn. *Moksha* is the highest stage a Buddhist soul can achieve. The Catholic equivalent might be sainthood.

It's nearing seven o'clock now and I'm bringing my *tommes* into the cellar. My cave is a room five feet under earth, lined in stone. Faith brings me here this morning with these *tommes,* faith that trusts in their refinement in the months to come. It's the same kind of faith that makes squirrels stash acorns underground and beavers drag branches into ponds for winter, and all animals prepare for what's to come. The same faith of the writer who takes decades to perfect her craft, and carve from all that time just one book.

I place the *tommes* on their shelves and leave them there with the others. And now begins the slow accumulation of hours, the months of aging and drying and refining. I'll turn and wash these *tommes* two or three times a week, and the months will slip and fade, and the *tommes* will sit in silence beneath the earth. They'll weep. They'll turn blue with penicillins, red with *Brevibacterium linens*. Black with *Mucor.* Each week a different color will shade their skin, browns and yellows and whites and purples, while inside a world is going on unseen. And each week new flowers will bloom on their faces, flora too small to see. And they will be like meadows, like fields, like grasslands with one growth coming and another dying—constantly in bloom.

As for my own *affinage,* I'm not so certain. All I can try to perfect in this lifetime is a cheese and maybe, if lucky, a book. My soul, though, will have to wait. I don't live in a concrete cell on top of a mountain or make a disciplined practice. I catch what I can now and then and sometimes my soul is here and sometimes it's not home. Even saints struggle toward perfection. Maybe that's what makes humans so endearing, that our souls are so imperfectible, even those who spend a lifetime to that end. That unlike other animals, humans struggle to achieve *just being*.

A cheese, a book, a soul—body, mind, spirit—do I really have to choose between one or the other? Can't I have all, be all, at once?

It's 6:59 on a Monday morning in late July. The day has already begun. I've got to go and milk the goats. Any second now the bells at the Charterhouse of the Transfiguration will bring me back. The monastery bells will ring Adoration in the church. I'm waiting in the basement at the bottom of this valley in western Vermont—my heart on hold. The time has come. Any second now, the bells. I've been waiting my whole life to hear them.

Artisanal

I MADE SEVERAL *TOMMES* THAT YEAR. THEY SAT ON SPRUCE boards in the cellar. The first wheels looked unpromising. During the hottest days of August they sweated a red bacterial slime—the coryneform bacterium *B. linens*—and reeked powerfully of ammonia. I wiped their rinds every few days with salt water and a cloth and patted them dry with paper towels. I set a fan in the cave to circulate air. The initial *tommes* were like the first batch of pancakes; they never quite formed the proper crust. Perhaps my cave hadn't built up enough of the right microorganisms. That would take time. I ended up giving the first wheels to the neighbor's pigs.

Each week that fall I watched the progress of the *tommes*. They turned blue at first and then peach, just like Caroline Gatti's *tommes* in France. By October they developed an impressive hard rind. Some had a beautiful nut brown finish while others turned the color of straw or winter wheat. When we sliced into one the interior was ivory—the color of old piano keys. The eyelets were small and well formed and the taste surprisingly good—savory and redolent of a freshly scythed meadow.

•

Friends came over to try the *tomme*. *Complex* was the word they used. They said it tasted exactly like a cheese they'd once had in France or Spain or Norway—they could never get more specific. I was too close to the *tomme* to be objective or use critical language on it. Was it really as good as we thought?

On a whim I called a Manhattan restaurant known for its handcrafted cheeses from around the world. I'd eaten at Artisanal once before and struck up a conversation with the *formagier.* That autumn we had to spend a night in New York City and I wondered if someone at the restaurant would try our *tomme* and give it an honest assessment. The woman at the cheese counter made no promise. If the cheese manager was there and not too busy, perhaps he'd give it a taste.

A week later, we arrived in Manhattan on a rainy October afternoon. The late lunch crowd had just left the restaurant, and busboys were setting silver for the evening meal. A dark-haired woman in a trim white cap stood at the cheese counter busily wrapping a Pont l'Évêque. Behind her a tall young man in a white uniform was talking on the phone. After a wait at the bar, the woman summoned Dona and me to the cheese counter. The young man—the manager—was all business at first. Dona brought out the *tomme* from a canvas sack. It was wrapped in brown paper tied in a hex of garden twine. Sean, the manager, undid the wrapping and exposed the wheel and the sprigs of lavender I'd placed against the rind. Chantal, the woman in the cap, clasped hands together and said it looked just like the rustic *fermier* cheese she grew up with in France.

The *tomme* was chestnut brown and slightly mottled. Sean made cuts with a knife and extracted a perfect wedge. He sniffed the cheese; its interior was bone white and firm. He inhaled and nodded slightly, then held the cheese to Chantal's nose and she nodded too. Then he cut some slices and they each took a taste and chewed and their nods grew larger. They swallowed, looked at each other, smiled, and Sean turned to us and said, "It's pretty good. Actually, it's *very* good."

The rest I don't remember, only that it suddenly seemed we were all good friends. Sean and Chantal tasted more cheese and used words like *herbaceous* and *grassy* and *nuts,* and we tasted the *tomme* too. Before we left I asked if Sean would give me language for the cheese. What did the *tomme taste* like? Sean said yes, he'd offer some language; he was great with the language of cheese.

The next morning a message arrived on the computer from Sean Faeth (his name was faith!) from Artisanal. He wrote:

> To describe your cheese—which I enjoyed very much—I would say: It has a nutty aroma. The palate is slightly eggy on the attack followed by grassy and herbaceous notes with a touch of white pepper spice and an undertone reminiscent of olives. These savory flavors meld beautifully with buttery notes of sweet cream followed by a hint of salt and mild goaty notes. The texture is yielding and slightly crumbly and the finish is long and savory. On the whole this cheese shows its roots in French Mountain style tommes, but is unique and firmly rooted in the American Farmstead tradition. It is a beautiful example of a lovingly hand crafted product, and should prove to be intriguing in many stages of its life. If you decide to go forward with getting licensed, I would love to carry this cheese.

Epilogue

WE BUILT A NEW BARN IN THE FALL OF THAT YEAR. Penny and Eustace Tilley were almost two and they'd have their own kids the following spring. The old chicken coop was just too small, especially with six expectant does. I drew up a plan for the barn based on the vernacular of ones nearby. Dona's brother and his family drove eight hours each weekend to help raise the barn. Each day we worked until dusk, sinking poles, hammering headers, raising rafters, as the trees around us lost their leaves. I didn't know at first that our barn design was a classical basilica, with a clerestory, nave, and two aisles. Yet when the framing was up and the first wall nailed in place, we all stood back and realized we were raising a cathedral.

That winter Mary Beth Bolduc had to sell her herd. We took in her aging matriarch, Alice-of-Jewel. She was Lizzie and Nisa's dam and the biggest and best-looking doe we'd ever seen, formidable at the age of ten and—it turned out—pregnant.

In the spring we birthed twelve kids, and with seven milking does, we were making too much cheese to eat and give away. We decided to try and get licensed to sell our *tommes*. I didn't want to sneak around with contraband wheels of cheese; and the process of getting licensed proved illuminating. It made us better cheesemakers.

Two state inspectors came to our house (one for the barn, the other for the "milk plant"). They made lists of things for us to do: whitewash the barn, seal the spring, make a bulk tank from our deep freeze, screw self-closers to the door . . . the lists went on. I poured a concrete floor in the cheese cave, faced its ceiling and walls with fiberglass-reinforced plastic panels, installed new lights and shelves for the *tommes*.

Trade curses everything it touches, wrote Thoreau, and I didn't want trade in cheese to curse what I loved. Our relationship with the goats—the milkings and cheesemaking—seemed intimate and holy. We made cheese because the goats gave us beautiful milk and the cheese fed us, not because I ever wanted to sell cheese. We never wished to milk more than a few goats (and already we were up to seven milkers). More goats would require a milking machine and a larger cheese vat, and there'd be more manure and more parasites and everyone would suffer—the animals and us. Largeness curses everything too; smallness was key. Could we keep the balance and trade a few wheels of cheese? We have yet to find that out.

It's February as I write this. The sun has not yet risen and the outside thermometer reads minus two. Snow has been drifting all night. Nine goats now lie in the barn—seven does and two kids we kept from last year's breeding out of Lizzie and Alice-of-Jewel. We kept them because we like their line, and it was time to start thinking about the future.

The house is cold this morning and I'm wearing two sweaters and a wool cap while I write. I'll wait until the dark lifts before heading to the barn. The does will be bedded on hay. They won't rise on such a bitter morning, but will wait for me to come and greet them, and each will give a soft moan in reply. They'll be chewing their cud, sister lying with sister; six of them with kids inside their wombs.

Downstairs the windows are cataracts of ice. I open the woodstove damper and place fresh kindling on the coals. I turn the kettle on in the kitchen, take a quarter wheel of *tomme* from the fridge, and cut a few triangles of cheese. We make art with paper, but now we make it with earth as well. A tome and a *tomme.* What began as a way to feed ourselves became in time a way to feed others. The cheese I place inside myself this morning is the grass from last July, the *journeywork of the stars,* the mineral extension of the does lying in the barn. This is their body. This is their work—Hannah and Lizzie, Nisa and Pie, Eustace and Alice and Penny. The tea is ready now. I pour a piping cup, place cheese on my tongue, and take—communion.

A goat has led me here. I'm the boy in the Yiddish tale who's followed her all along—she always knew the way back home.

Wind catches the eaves. The light comes up, a brown incandescence in the east. In the cave our *tommes* are almost all consumed, the shelves nearly empty. We've eaten all the books page by page; my wheel, my depth, my volume—complete.

let's stop here and sing our songs.
Put down the baby goats; we'll make it to town:
Or if you're afraid it's going to rain tonight,
Let's keep on going, but singing as we go.
Singing makes the journey easier.
I'll carry the basket awhile, so you can sing.

—VIRGIL, *ECLOGUE IX*

I wish to thank Mary Beth Bolduc, Melvin and Jennifer Lawrence, Dottie Cross, Jean Eisenhart, Peter Dixon, Caroline Gatti, Michel Terret, Kim Chevalier, Carol Delaney, Steve McAdams, Eve and Phil Maynard, Bill Clary, Suzy and Valerie dePeyster, Alice Gordon, Mona Talbott, Joanne Ahola, Isabel and Stuart Kessler, the Granville Large Animal Veterinary Practice, Nancy Zafris, Lisa Dickey, Stephen Hubbell, David Baker, Susan Taylor Chehak, Chris Abani, Suzanne Gardinier, Paul Whitlatch, and Betsy Lerner. Gratitude to Nan Graham for her continual editorial brilliance and for the special *affinage* this tome required. I owe a great debt to the Giles Whiting Foundation, the American Academy of Arts and Letters, and the American Academy in Rome. Thank you. As always, to Dona, first and last reader.